I0003323

Draft NIST Special Publication 800-171

Revision 2

Protecting Controlled Unclassified Information in Nonfederal Systems and Organizations

RON ROSS
VICTORIA PILLITTERI
KELLEY DEMPSEY
MARK RIDDLE
GARY GUISSANIE

National Institute of
Standards and Technology
U.S. Department of Commerce

Draft NIST Special Publication 800-171
Revision 2

Protecting Controlled Unclassified Information in Nonfederal Systems and Organizations

RON ROSS
VICTORIA PILLITTERI
KELLEY DEMPSEY
Computer Security Division
National Institute of Standards and Technology

MARK RIDDLE
Information Security Oversight Office
National Archives and Records Administration

GARY GUISSANIE
Institute for Defense Analyses

June 2019

U.S. Department of Commerce
Wilbur L. Ross, Jr., Secretary

National Institute of Standards and Technology
Walter Copan, NIST Director and Under Secretary of Commerce for Standards and Technology

Authority

This publication has been developed by NIST to further its statutory responsibilities under the Federal Information Security Modernization Act (FISMA), 44 U.S.C. § 3551 *et seq.*, Public Law (P.L.) 113-283. NIST is responsible for developing information security standards and guidelines, including minimum requirements for federal information systems, but such standards and guidelines shall not apply to national security systems without the express approval of the appropriate federal officials exercising policy authority over such systems. This guideline is consistent with requirements of the Office of Management and Budget (OMB) Circular A-130.

Nothing in this publication should be taken to contradict the standards and guidelines made mandatory and binding on federal agencies by the Secretary of Commerce under statutory authority. Nor should these guidelines be interpreted as altering or superseding the existing authorities of the Secretary of Commerce, OMB Director, or any other federal official. This publication may be used by nongovernmental organizations on a voluntary basis and is not subject to copyright in the United States. Attribution would, however, be appreciated by NIST.

National Institute of Standards and Technology Special Publication 800-171, Revision 2
Natl. Inst. Stand. Technol. Spec. Publ. 800-171, Rev. 2, **121 pages** (June 2019)

CODEN: NSPUE2

Public comment period: June 19 through July 19, 2019

National Institute of Standards and Technology
Attn: Computer Security Division, Information Technology Laboratory
100 Bureau Drive (Mail Stop 8930) Gaithersburg, MD 20899-8930
Email: sec-cert@nist.gov

All comments are subject to release under the Freedom of Information Act (FOIA) [FOIA96].

Reports on Computer Systems Technology

The National Institute of Standards and Technology (NIST) Information Technology Laboratory (ITL) promotes the U.S. economy and public welfare by providing technical leadership for the Nation's measurement and standards infrastructure. ITL develops tests, test methods, reference data, proof of concept implementations, and technical analyses to advance the development and productive use of information technology (IT). ITL's responsibilities include the development of management, administrative, technical, and physical standards and guidelines for the cost-effective security of other than national security-related information in federal information systems. The Special Publication 800-series reports on ITL's research, guidelines, and outreach efforts in information systems security and privacy and its collaborative activities with industry, government, and academic organizations.

Abstract

The protection of Controlled Unclassified Information (CUI) resident in nonfederal systems and organizations is of paramount importance to federal agencies and can directly impact the ability of the federal government to successfully conduct its essential missions and functions. This publication provides agencies with recommended security requirements for protecting the confidentiality of CUI when the information is resident in nonfederal systems and organizations; when the nonfederal organization is not collecting or maintaining information on behalf of a federal agency or using or operating a system on behalf of an agency; and where there are no specific safeguarding requirements for protecting the confidentiality of CUI prescribed by the authorizing law, regulation, or governmentwide policy for the CUI category listed in the CUI Registry. The requirements apply to all components of nonfederal systems and organizations that process, store, or transmit CUI, or that provide security protection for such components. The requirements are intended for use by federal agencies in contractual vehicles or other agreements established between those agencies and nonfederal organizations.

Keywords

Basic Security Requirement; Contractor Systems; Controlled Unclassified Information; CUI Registry; Derived Security Requirement; Executive Order 13556; FIPS Publication 199; FIPS Publication 200; FISMA; NIST Special Publication 800-53; Nonfederal Organizations; Nonfederal Systems; Security Assessment; Security Control; Security Requirement.

Acknowledgements

The authors also wish to recognize the scientists, engineers, and research staff from the NIST Computer Security and the Applied Cybersecurity Divisions for their exceptional contributions in helping to improve the content of the publication. A special note of thanks to Pat O'Reilly, Jim Foti, Jeff Brewer and the NIST web team for their outstanding administrative support. Finally, the authors also gratefully acknowledge the contributions from individuals and organizations in the public and private sectors, nationally and internationally, whose thoughtful and constructive comments improved the overall quality, thoroughness, and usefulness of this publication.

HISTORICAL CONTRIBUTIONS TO NIST SPECIAL PUBLICATION 800-171

The authors acknowledge the many individuals who contributed to previous versions of Special Publication 800-171 since its inception in June 2015. They include Carol Bales, Matthew Barrett, Jon Boyens, Devin Casey, Kelley Dempsey, Christian Enloe, Peggy Himes, Robert Glenn, Elizabeth Lennon, Vicki Michetti, Dorian Pappas, Karen Quigg, Mary Thomas, Matthew Scholl, Murugiah Souppaya, Patricia Toth, and Patrick Viscuso.

Notes to Reviewers

This update provides minor editorial changes in Chapter One, Chapter Two, and the Glossary, Acronyms, and list of References. **There are no changes to the basic and derived security requirements in** <u>**Chapter Three**</u>. For ease of use, the Discussion sections, previously located in Appendix F, have be relocated to Chapter Three to coincide with the basic and derived security requirements. A comprehensive update to this publication (including updates to the basic and derived requirements) will be forthcoming in Revision 3 following the issuance of NIST Special Publication 800-53, Revision 5, which will include modified control families, privacy integration, and make other conforming edits that are necessary.

Your feedback is important to us. We appreciate each contribution from our reviewers. The very insightful comments from the public and private sectors, nationally and internationally, continue to help shape the final publication to ensure that it meets the needs and expectations of our customers.

-   **RON ROSS**
    NATIONAL INSTITUTE OF STANDARDS AND TECHNOLOGY

Call for Patent Claims

This public review includes a call for information on essential patent claims (claims whose use would be required for compliance with the guidance or requirements in this Information Technology Laboratory (ITL) draft publication). Such guidance and/or requirements may be directly stated in this ITL Publication or by reference to another publication. This call includes disclosure, where known, of the existence of pending U.S. or foreign patent applications relating to this ITL draft publication and of any relevant unexpired U.S. or foreign patents.

ITL may require from the patent holder, or a party authorized to make assurances on its behalf, in written or electronic form, either:

a) assurance in the form of a general disclaimer to the effect that such party does not hold and does not currently intend holding any essential patent claim(s); or

b) assurance that a license to such essential patent claim(s) will be made available to applicants desiring to utilize the license for the purpose of complying with the guidance or requirements in this ITL draft publication either:

    i) under reasonable terms and conditions that are demonstrably free of any unfair discrimination; or

    ii) without compensation and under reasonable terms and conditions that are demonstrably free of any unfair discrimination.

Such assurance shall indicate that the patent holder (or third party authorized to make assurances on its behalf) will include in any documents transferring ownership of patents subject to the assurance, provisions sufficient to ensure that the commitments in the assurance are binding on the transferee, and that the transferee will similarly include appropriate provisions in the event of future transfers with the goal of binding each successor-in-interest.

The assurance shall also indicate that it is intended to be binding on successors-in-interest regardless of whether such provisions are included in the relevant transfer documents.

Such statements should be addressed to: sec-cert@nist.gov.

CAUTIONARY NOTE

The Federal Information Security Modernization Act [FISMA] of 2014 requires federal agencies to identify and provide information security protections commensurate with the risk resulting from the unauthorized access, use, disclosure, disruption, modification, or destruction of information collected or maintained by or on behalf of an agency; or information systems used or operated by an agency or by a contractor of an agency or other organization on behalf of an agency. This publication focuses on protecting the *confidentiality* of Controlled Unclassified Information (CUI) in *nonfederal* systems and organizations and recommends specific security requirements to achieve that objective. It does not change the requirements set forth in FISMA, nor does it alter the responsibility of federal agencies to comply with the full provisions of the statute, the policies established by OMB, and the supporting security standards and guidelines developed by NIST.

The requirements recommended for use in this publication are derived from [FIPS 200] and the moderate security control baseline in [SP 800-53] and are based on the CUI regulation [32 CFR 2002]. The requirements and controls have been determined over time to provide the necessary protection for federal information and systems that are covered under FISMA. The tailoring criteria applied to the [FIPS 200] requirements and [SP 800-53] controls is *not* an endorsement for the elimination of those requirements and controls—rather, the tailoring criteria focuses on the protection of CUI from unauthorized disclosure in nonfederal systems and organizations. Moreover, since the security requirements are derivative from the NIST publications listed above, organizations should *not* assume that satisfying those particular requirements will automatically satisfy the security requirements and controls in [FIPS 200] and [SP 800-53].

In addition to the security objective of *confidentiality*, the objectives of *integrity* and *availability* remain a high priority for organizations that are concerned with establishing and maintaining a comprehensive information security program. While the primary purpose of this publication is to define requirements to protect the confidentiality of CUI, there is a close relationship between confidentiality and integrity since many of the underlying security mechanisms at the system level support both security objectives. Therefore, the basic and derived security requirements in this publication provide protection from unauthorized disclosure and unauthorized modification of CUI. Organizations that are interested in or required to comply with the recommendations in this publication are strongly advised to review the complete listing of controls in the moderate baseline in Appendix E to ensure that their individual security plans and control deployments provide the necessary and sufficient protection to address the cyber and kinetic threats to organizational missions and business operations.

CUI SECURITY REQUIREMENTS

The recommended security requirements contained in this publication are only *applicable* for a nonfederal system or organization when *mandated* by a federal agency in a contract, grant, or other agreement. The requirements apply only to the components of nonfederal systems that process, store, or transmit CUI, or that provide security protection for such components.

FRAMEWORK FOR IMPROVING CRITICAL INFRASTRUCTURE CYBERSECURITY

Organizations that have implemented or plan to implement the NIST *Framework for Improving Critical Infrastructure Cybersecurity* [NIST CSF] can find in Appendix D, a direct mapping of the Controlled Unclassified Information (CUI) security requirements to the security controls in [SP 800-53] and [ISO 27001]. These controls are also mapped to the Categories and Subcategories associated with Cybersecurity Framework Core Functions: *Identify, Protect, Detect, Respond,* and *Recover.* The security control mappings can be useful to organizations that wish to demonstrate compliance to the security requirements in the context of their established information security programs, when such programs have been built around the NIST or ISO/IEC security controls.

ADDITIONAL RESOURCES

Mapping security controls to the Cybersecurity Framework:
https://www.nist.gov/file/372651.

Mapping CUI security requirements to the Cybersecurity Framework:
https://csrc.nist.gov/publications/detail/sp/800-171/rev-1/final.

Table of Contents

Errata

This table contains changes that have been incorporated into Special Publication 800-171. Errata updates can include corrections, clarifications, or other minor changes in the publication that are either *editorial* or *substantive* in nature.

DATE	TYPE	CHANGE	PAGE

CHAPTER ONE

INTRODUCTION

THE NEED TO PROTECT CONTROLLED UNCLASSIFIED INFORMATION

Today, more than at any time in history, the federal government is relying on external service providers to help carry out a wide range of federal missions and business functions using information systems.[1] Many federal contractors, for example, routinely process, store, and transmit sensitive federal information in their systems to support the delivery of essential products and services to federal agencies (e.g., financial services; providing Web and electronic mail services; processing security clearances or healthcare data; providing cloud services; and developing communications, satellite, and weapons systems). Federal information is frequently provided to or shared with entities such as State and local governments, colleges and universities, and independent research organizations. The protection of sensitive federal information while residing in *nonfederal systems*[2] and organizations is of paramount importance to federal agencies and can directly impact the ability of the federal government to carry out its designated missions and business operations.

The protection of unclassified federal information in nonfederal systems and organizations is dependent on the federal government providing a process for identifying the different types of information that are used by federal agencies. [EO 13556] established a governmentwide Controlled Unclassified Information (CUI)[3] Program to standardize the way the executive branch handles unclassified information that requires protection.[4] Only information that requires safeguarding or dissemination controls pursuant to federal law, regulation, or governmentwide policy may be designated as CUI. The CUI Program is designed to address several deficiencies in managing and protecting unclassified information to include inconsistent markings, inadequate safeguarding, and needless restrictions, both by standardizing procedures and by providing common definitions through a CUI Registry [NARA CUI]. The CUI Registry is the online repository for information, guidance, policy, and requirements on handling CUI, including issuances by the CUI Executive Agent. The CUI Registry identifies approved CUI categories, provides general descriptions for each, identifies the basis for controls, and sets out procedures for the use of CUI, including but not limited to marking, safeguarding, transporting, disseminating, reusing, and disposing of the information.

---

[1] An *information system* is a discrete set of information resources organized expressly for the collection, processing, maintenance, use, sharing, dissemination, or disposition of information. Information systems also include specialized systems for example, industrial/process control systems, cyber-physical systems, embedded systems, and devices. The term *system* is used throughout this publication to represent all types of computing platforms that can process, store, or transmit CUI.

[2] A *federal information system* is a system that is used or operated by an executive agency, by a contractor of an executive agency, or by another organization on behalf of an executive agency. A system that does not meet such criteria is a *nonfederal system*.

[3] *Controlled Unclassified Information* is any information that law, regulation, or governmentwide policy requires to have safeguarding or disseminating controls, excluding information that is classified under [EO 13526] or any predecessor or successor order, or [ATOM54], as amended.

[4] [EO 13526] designated the National Archives and Records Administration (NARA) as the Executive Agent to implement the CUI program.

[EO 13556] also required that the CUI Program emphasize openness, transparency, and uniformity of governmentwide practices, and that the implementation of the program take place in a manner consistent with applicable policies established by the Office of Management and Budget (OMB) and federal standards and guidelines issued by the National Institute of Standards and Technology (NIST). The federal CUI *regulation*,[5] developed by the CUI Executive Agent, provides guidance to federal agencies on the designation, safeguarding, dissemination, marking, decontrolling, and disposition of CUI, establishes self-inspection and oversight requirements, and delineates other facets of the program.

1.1 PURPOSE AND APPLICABILITY

The purpose of this publication is to provide federal agencies with recommended security requirements[6] for protecting the *confidentiality* of CUI: (1) when the CUI is resident in a nonfederal system and organization; (2) when the nonfederal organization is *not* collecting or maintaining information on behalf of a federal agency or using or operating a system on behalf of an agency;[7] and (3) where there are no specific safeguarding requirements for protecting the confidentiality of CUI prescribed by the authorizing law, regulation, or governmentwide policy for the CUI category listed in the CUI Registry.[8] The requirements apply *only* to components of nonfederal systems that process, store, or transmit CUI, or that provide security protection for such components.[9] The requirements are intended for use by federal agencies in appropriate contractual vehicles or other agreements established between those agencies and nonfederal organizations. In CUI guidance and the CUI Federal Acquisition Regulation (FAR),[10] the CUI Executive Agent will address determining compliance with security requirements.[11]

---

[5] [32 CFR 2002] was issued on September 14, 2016 and became effective on November 14, 2016.

[6] The term *requirements* can be used in different contexts. In the context of federal information security and privacy policies, the term is generally used to refer to information security and privacy obligations imposed on organizations. For example, OMB Circular A-130 imposes a series of information security and privacy requirements with which federal agencies must comply when managing information resources. In addition to the use of the term requirements in the context of federal policy, the term requirements is used in this guideline in a broader sense to refer to an expression of the set of stakeholder protection needs for a particular system or organization. Stakeholder protection needs and corresponding security requirements may be derived from many sources (e.g., laws, executive orders, directives, regulations, policies, standards, mission and business needs, or risk assessments). The term requirements, as used in this guideline, includes both legal and policy requirements, as well as an expression of the broader set of stakeholder protection needs that may be derived from other sources. All of these requirements, when applied to a system, help determine the required characteristics of the system.

[7] Nonfederal organizations that collect or maintain information *on behalf of* a federal agency or that use or operate a system *on behalf of* an agency, must comply with the requirements in FISMA, including the requirements in [FIPS 200] and the security controls in [SP 800-53] (See [44 USC 3554] (a)(1)(A)).

[8] The requirements in this publication can be used to comply with the FISMA requirement for senior agency officials to provide information security for the information that supports the operations and assets under their control, including CUI that is resident in nonfederal systems and organizations (See [44 USC 3554] (a)(1)(A) and (a)(2)).

[9] System *components* include, for example: mainframes, workstations, servers; input and output devices; network components; operating systems; virtual machines; and applications.

[10] NARA, in its capacity as the CUI Executive Agent, plans to sponsor in 2019, a single FAR clause that will apply the requirements of the federal CUI regulation and NIST Special Publication 800-171 to contractors. Until the FAR clause is in place, the requirements in NIST Special Publication 800-171 may be referenced in federal contracts consistent with federal law and regulatory requirements.

[11] [SP 800-171A] provides assessment procedures to determine compliance to the CUI security requirements.

In accordance with the federal CUI regulation, federal agencies using federal systems to process, store, or transmit CUI, as a minimum, must comply with:

- Federal Information Processing Standards (FIPS) Publication 199, *Standards for Security Categorization of Federal Information and Information Systems* (moderate confidentiality);[12]

- Federal Information Processing Standards (FIPS) Publication 200, *Minimum Security Requirements for Federal Information and Information Systems*;

- NIST Special Publication 800-53, *Security and Privacy Controls for Federal Information Systems and Organizations*; and

- NIST Special Publication 800-60, *Guide for Mapping Types of Information and Information Systems to Security Categories.*

The responsibility of federal agencies to protect CUI does not change when such information is shared with nonfederal partners. Therefore, a similar level of protection is needed when CUI is processed, stored, or transmitted by *nonfederal organizations* using nonfederal systems.[13] The recommended requirements for safeguarding CUI in nonfederal systems and organizations are derived from the above authoritative federal standards and guidelines to maintain a consistent level of protection. However, recognizing that the scope of the safeguarding requirements in the federal CUI regulation is limited to the security objective of confidentiality (i.e., not directly addressing integrity and availability) and that some of the security requirements expressed in the NIST standards and guidelines are uniquely federal, the requirements in this publication have been *tailored* for nonfederal entities.

The tailoring criteria, described in Chapter Two, are not intended to reduce or minimize the federal requirements for the safeguarding of CUI as expressed in the federal CUI regulation. Rather, the intent is to express the requirements in a manner that allows for and facilitates the equivalent safeguarding measures within nonfederal systems and organizations and does not diminish the level of protection of CUI required for moderate confidentiality. Additional or differing requirements, other than the requirements described in this publication, may be applied only when such requirements are based on law, regulation, or governmentwide policy and when indicated in the CUI Registry as CUI-specified or when an agreement establishes requirements to protect CUI Basic[14] at higher than moderate confidentiality. The provision of safeguarding requirements for CUI in a specified category will be addressed by NARA in its CUI guidance and in the CUI FAR; and reflected as specific requirements in contracts or other agreements.

If nonfederal organizations entrusted with protecting CUI designate systems or components for the processing, storage, or transmission of CUI, those organizations may limit the scope of the security requirements to only those systems or components. Isolating CUI into its own *security domain* by applying architectural design concepts (e.g., implementing subnetworks with firewalls or other boundary protection devices) may be the most cost-effective and efficient

---

[12] [FIPS 199] defines three values of potential impact (i.e., low, moderate, high) on organizations, assets, or individuals in the event of a breach of security (e.g., a loss of confidentiality).

[13] A *nonfederal organization* is any entity that owns, operates, or maintains a nonfederal system. Examples include: State, local, and tribal governments; colleges and universities; and contractors.

[14] CUI Basic is defined in the CUI Registry [NARA CUI].

approach for nonfederal organizations to satisfy the security requirements and protect the confidentiality of CUI. Security domains may employ physical separation, logical separation, or a combination of both. This approach can reasonably provide adequate security for the CUI and avoid increasing the organization's security posture to a level beyond which it typically requires for protecting its missions, operations, and assets. Nonfederal organizations may use the same CUI infrastructure for multiple government contracts or agreements, if the CUI infrastructure meets the safeguarding requirements for the organization's CUI-related contracts and/or agreements including any specific safeguarding required or permitted by the authorizing law, regulation, or governmentwide policy.

1.2 TARGET AUDIENCE

This publication serves a diverse group of individuals and organizations in both the public and private sectors including, but not limited to individuals with:

- System development life cycle responsibilities (e.g., program managers, mission/business owners, information owners/stewards, system designers and developers, system/security engineers, systems integrators);

- Acquisition or procurement responsibilities (e.g., contracting officers);

- System, security, or risk management and oversight responsibilities (e.g., authorizing officials, chief information officers, chief information security officers, system owners, information security managers); and

- Security assessment and monitoring responsibilities (e.g., auditors, system evaluators, assessors, independent verifiers/validators, analysts).

The above roles and responsibilities can be viewed from two distinct perspectives: the *federal perspective* as the entity establishing and conveying the security requirements in contractual vehicles or other types of inter-organizational agreements; and the *nonfederal perspective* as the entity responding to and complying with the security requirements set forth in contracts or agreements.

1.3 ORGANIZATION OF THIS SPECIAL PUBLICATION

The remainder of this special publication is organized as follows:

- Chapter Two describes the fundamental assumptions and methodology used to develop the security requirements for protecting the confidentiality of CUI; the format and structure of the requirements; and the tailoring criteria applied to the NIST standards and guidelines to obtain the requirements.

- Chapter Three describes the fourteen families of security requirements for protecting the confidentiality of CUI in nonfederal systems and organizations.

- Supporting appendices provide additional information related to the protection of CUI in nonfederal systems and organizations including: general references; definitions and terms; acronyms; mapping tables relating security requirements to the security controls in [SP 800-53] and [ISO 27001]; and tailoring actions applied to the moderate security control baseline.

CHAPTER TWO

THE FUNDAMENTALS

ASSUMPTIONS AND METHODOLOGY FOR DEVELOPING SECURITY REQUIREMENTS

This chapter describes the assumptions and the methodology used to develop the recommended security requirements to protect CUI in nonfederal systems and organizations; the structure of the basic and derived security requirements; and the tailoring criteria applied to the federal information security requirements and controls.

2.1 BASIC ASSUMPTIONS

The recommended security requirements described in this publication have been developed based on three fundamental assumptions:

- Statutory and regulatory requirements for the protection of CUI are *consistent*, whether such information resides in federal systems or nonfederal systems including the environments in which those systems operate;

- Safeguards implemented to protect CUI are *consistent* in both federal and nonfederal systems and organizations; and

- The confidentiality impact value for CUI is no less than [FIPS 199] *moderate*.[15] [16]

The assumptions reinforce the concept that federal information designated as CUI has the same intrinsic *value* and potential *adverse impact* if compromised—whether such information resides in a federal or a nonfederal organization. Thus, protecting the confidentiality of CUI is critical to the mission and business success of federal agencies and the economic and national security interests of the nation. Additional assumptions also impacting the development of the security requirements and the expectation of federal agencies in working with nonfederal entities include:

- Nonfederal organizations have information technology infrastructures in place, and are not necessarily developing or acquiring systems specifically for processing, storing, or transmitting CUI;

- Nonfederal organizations have specific safeguarding measures in place to protect their information which may also be sufficient to satisfy the security requirements;

- Nonfederal organizations may not have the necessary organizational structure or resources to satisfy every security requirement and may implement alternative, but equally effective, security measures to compensate for the inability to satisfy a requirement; and

- Nonfederal organizations can implement a variety of potential security solutions directly or using external service providers (e.g., managed services), to satisfy security requirements.

---

[15] The moderate impact *value* defined in [FIPS 199] may become part of a moderate impact *system* in [FIPS 200], which requires the use of the moderate baseline in [SP 800-53] as the starting point for tailoring actions.

[16] In accordance with [32 CFR 2002], CUI is categorized at no less than the moderate confidentiality impact value. However, when federal law, regulation, or governmentwide policy establishing the control of the CUI specifies controls that differ from those of the moderate confidentiality baseline, then these will be followed.

IMPLEMENTING A SINGLE STATE SECURITY SOLUTION FOR CUI

Controlled Unclassified Information has the *same value*, whether such information is resident in a federal system that is part of a federal agency or a nonfederal system that is part of a nonfederal organization. Accordingly, the recommended security requirements contained in this publication are consistent with and are complementary to the standards and guidelines used by federal agencies to protect CUI.

2.2 DEVELOPMENT OF SECURITY REQUIREMENTS

The security requirements for protecting the confidentiality of CUI in nonfederal systems and organizations have a well-defined structure that consists of a *basic security requirements* section and a *derived security requirements* section. The basic security requirements are obtained from [FIPS 200], which provides the high-level and fundamental security requirements for federal information and systems. The derived security requirements, which supplement the basic security requirements, are taken from the security controls in [SP 800-53]. Starting with the security requirements and the security controls in the moderate baseline (i.e., the minimum level of protection required for CUI in federal systems and organizations), the requirements and controls are *tailored* to eliminate requirements, controls, or parts of controls that are:

- Uniquely federal (i.e., primarily the responsibility of the federal government);

- Not directly related to protecting the confidentiality of CUI; or

- Expected to be routinely satisfied by nonfederal organizations without specification.[17]

Appendix E provides a complete listing of security controls that support the CUI derived security requirements and those controls that have been eliminated from the moderate baseline based on the CUI tailoring criteria described above.

The combination of the basic and derived security requirements captures the intent of [FIPS 200] and [SP 800-53], with respect to the protection of the *confidentiality* of CUI in nonfederal systems and organizations. Appendix D provides informal mappings of the security requirements to the relevant security controls in [SP 800-53] and [ISO 27001]. The mappings promote a better understanding of the CUI security requirements and are *not* intended to impose additional requirements on nonfederal organizations.

---

[17] The security requirements developed from the tailored [FIPS 200] security requirements and the [SP 800-53] moderate security control baseline represent a subset of the safeguarding measures that are necessary for a *comprehensive* information security program. The strength and quality of such programs in nonfederal organizations depend on the degree to which the organizations implement the security requirements and controls that are expected to be routinely satisfied without specification by the federal government. This includes implementing security policies, procedures, and practices that support an effective risk-based information security program. Nonfederal organizations are encouraged to refer to Appendix E and [SP 800-53] for a complete listing of security controls in the moderate baseline deemed out of scope for the security requirements in Chapter Three.

The following *Media Protection* family example illustrates the structure of a CUI requirement:

Basic Security Requirements

3.8.1   Protect (i.e., physically control and securely store) system media containing CUI, both paper and digital.

3.8.2   Limit access to CUI on system media to authorized users.

3.8.3   Sanitize or destroy system media containing CUI before disposal or release for reuse.

Derived Security Requirements

3.8.4   Mark media with necessary CUI markings and distribution limitations.

3.8.5   Control access to media containing CUI and maintain accountability for media during transport outside of controlled areas.

3.8.6   Implement cryptographic mechanisms to protect the confidentiality of CUI stored on digital media during transport unless otherwise protected by alternative physical safeguards.

3.8.7   Control the use of removable media on system components.

3.8.8   Prohibit the use of portable storage devices when such devices have no identifiable owner.

3.8.9   Protect the confidentiality of backup CUI at storage locations.

For ease of use, the security requirements are organized into fourteen *families*. Each family contains the requirements related to the general security topic of the family. The families are closely aligned with the minimum-security requirements for federal information and systems described in [FIPS 200]. The *contingency planning*, *system and services acquisition*, and *planning* requirements are not included within the scope of this publication due to the tailoring criteria.[18] Table 1 lists the security requirement families addressed in this publication.

TABLE 1: SECURITY REQUIREMENT FAMILIES

FAMILY	FAMILY
Access Control	Media Protection
Awareness and Training	Personnel Security
Audit and Accountability	Physical Protection
Configuration Management	Risk Assessment
Identification and Authentication	Security Assessment
Incident Response	System and Communications Protection
Maintenance	System and Information Integrity

---

[18] Three exceptions include: a requirement to protect the confidentiality of system backups (derived from CP-9) from the *contingency planning* family; a requirement to develop and implement a system security plan (derived from PL-2) from the *planning* family; and a requirement to implement system security engineering principles (derived from SA-8) from the *system and services acquisition* family. The requirements are included in the CUI *media protection*, *security assessment*, and *system and communications protection* requirements families, respectively.

A *discussion section* follows each CUI security requirement providing additional information to facilitate the implementation and assessment of the requirements. This information is derived primarily from the security controls discussion sections in [SP 800-53] and is provided to give organizations a better understanding of the mechanisms and procedures used to implement the controls used to protect CUI. The discussion section is not intended to extend the scope of the requirements. Figure 1 illustrates basic security requirement 3.8.3 with its supporting discussion section and informative references.

3.8.3   **Sanitize or destroy system media containing CUI before disposal or release for reuse.**

DISCUSSION

This requirement applies to all system media, digital and non-digital, subject to disposal or reuse. Examples include: digital media found in workstations, network components, scanners, copiers, printers, notebook computers, and mobile devices; and non-digital media such as paper and microfilm. The sanitization process removes information from the media such that the information cannot be retrieved or reconstructed. Sanitization techniques, including clearing, purging, cryptographic erase, and destruction, prevent the disclosure of information to unauthorized individuals when such media is released for reuse or disposal.

Organizations determine the appropriate sanitization methods, recognizing that destruction may be necessary when other methods cannot be applied to the media requiring sanitization. Organizations use discretion on the employment of sanitization techniques and procedures for media containing information that is in the public domain or publicly releasable or deemed to have no adverse impact on organizations or individuals if released for reuse or disposal. Sanitization of non-digital media includes destruction, removing CUI from documents, or redacting selected sections or words from a document by obscuring the redacted sections or words in a manner equivalent in effectiveness to removing the words or sections from the document. NARA policy and guidance control sanitization processes for controlled unclassified information.

[SP 800-88] provides guidance on media sanitization.

FIGURE 1: FORMAT AND STRUCTURE OF CUI SECURITY REQUIREMENT

CHAPTER THREE

THE REQUIREMENTS

SECURITY REQUIREMENTS FOR PROTECTING THE CONFIDENTIALITY OF CUI

This chapter describes fourteen families of recommended security requirements for protecting the confidentiality of CUI in nonfederal systems and organizations.[19] The security controls from [SP 800-53] associated with the basic and derived requirements are listed in Appendix D.[20] Organizations can use the NIST publication to obtain additional, non-prescriptive information related to the recommended security requirements (e.g., explanatory information in the discussion section for each of the referenced security controls, mapping tables to [ISO 27001] security controls, and a catalog of optional controls that can be used to specify additional security requirements, if needed).

This information can help clarify or interpret the requirements in the context of mission and business requirements, operational environments, or assessments of risk. Nonfederal organizations can implement a variety of potential security solutions either directly or using managed services, to satisfy the security requirements and may implement alternative, but equally effective, security measures to compensate for the inability to satisfy a requirement.[21]

Nonfederal organizations describe in a system security plan, how the security requirements are met or how organizations plan to meet the requirements and address known and anticipated threats. The system security plan describes the system boundary; operational environment; how security requirements are implemented; and the relationships with or connections to other systems. Nonfederal organizations develop plans of action that describe how unimplemented security requirements will be met and how any planned mitigations will be implemented. Organizations can document the system security plan and the plan of action as separate or combined documents and in any chosen format.[22]

When requested, the system security plan (or extracts thereof) and the associated plans of action for any planned implementations or mitigations are submitted to the responsible federal agency/contracting office to demonstrate the nonfederal organization's implementation or planned implementation of the security requirements. Federal agencies may consider the submitted system security plans and plans of action as critical inputs to a risk management decision to process, store, or transmit CUI on a system hosted by a nonfederal organization and whether it is advisable to pursue an agreement or contract with the nonfederal organization.

---

[19] The security objectives of confidentiality and integrity are closely related since many of the underlying security mechanisms at the system level support both objectives. Therefore, the basic and derived security requirements in this publication provide protection from unauthorized disclosure and unauthorized modification of CUI.

[20] The security control references in Appendix D are included to promote a better understanding of the recommended security requirements and do not expand the scope of the requirements.

[21] To promote consistency, transparency, and comparability, the compensatory security measures selected by organizations are based on or derived from *existing* and *recognized* security standards and control sets, including, for example, [ISO 27001] or [SP 800-53].

[22] [NIST CUI] provides supplemental material for Special Publication 800-171 including templates for system security plans and plans of action.

The recommended security requirements in this publication apply only to the components of nonfederal systems that process, store, or transmit CUI or that provide protection for such components. Some systems, including specialized systems (e.g., industrial/process control systems, medical devices, Computer Numerical Control machines), may have limitations on the application of certain security requirements.

To accommodate such issues, the system security plan, as reflected in Requirement 3.12.4, is used to describe any enduring exceptions to the security requirements. Individual, isolated, or temporary deficiencies are managed though plans of action, as reflected in Requirement 3.12.2.

THE MEANING OF ORGANIZATIONAL SYSTEMS

The term *organizational system* is used in many of the recommended CUI security requirements in this publication. This term has a specific meaning regarding the scope of applicability for the security requirements. The requirements apply only to the components of nonfederal systems that process, store, or transmit CUI, or that provide protection for the system components. The appropriate scoping for the CUI security requirements is an important factor in determining protection-related investment decisions and managing security risk for nonfederal organizations that have the responsibility of safeguarding CUI.

3.1 ACCESS CONTROL

Basic Security Requirements

3.1.1 **Limit system access to authorized users, processes acting on behalf of authorized users, and devices (including other systems).**

DISCUSSION

Access control policies (e.g., identity- or role-based policies, control matrices, and cryptography) control access between active entities or subjects (i.e., users or processes acting on behalf of users) and passive entities or objects (e.g., devices, files, records, and domains) in systems. Access enforcement mechanisms can be employed at the application and service level to provide increased information security. Other systems include systems internal and external to the organization. This requirement focuses on account management for systems and applications. The definition of and enforcement of access authorizations, other than those determined by account type (e.g., privileged verses non-privileged) are addressed in requirement 3.1.2.

3.1.2 **Limit system access to the types of transactions and functions that authorized users are permitted to execute.**

DISCUSSION

Organizations may choose to define access privileges or other attributes by account, by type of account, or a combination of both. System account types include individual, shared, group, system, anonymous, guest, emergency, developer, manufacturer, vendor, and temporary. Other attributes required for authorizing access include restrictions on time-of-day, day-of-week, and point-of-origin. In defining other account attributes, organizations consider system-related requirements (e.g., system upgrades scheduled maintenance,) and mission or business requirements, (e.g., time zone differences, customer requirements, remote access to support travel requirements).

Derived Security Requirements

3.1.3 **Control the flow of CUI in accordance with approved authorizations.**

DISCUSSION

Information flow control regulates where information can travel within a system and between systems (versus who can access the information) and without explicit regard to subsequent accesses to that information. Flow control restrictions include the following: keeping export-controlled information from being transmitted in the clear to the Internet; blocking outside traffic that claims to be from within the organization; restricting requests to the Internet that are not from the internal web proxy server; and limiting information transfers between organizations based on data structures and content.

Organizations commonly use information flow control policies and enforcement mechanisms to control the flow of information between designated sources and destinations (e.g., networks, individuals, and devices) within systems and between interconnected systems. Flow control is based on characteristics of the information or the information path. Enforcement occurs in boundary protection devices (e.g., gateways, routers, guards, encrypted tunnels, firewalls) that employ rule sets or establish configuration settings that restrict system services, provide a packet-filtering capability based on header information, or message-filtering capability based on message content (e.g., implementing key word searches or using document characteristics). Organizations also consider the trustworthiness of filtering and inspection mechanisms (i.e., hardware, firmware, and software components) that are critical to information flow enforcement.

Transferring information between systems representing different security domains with different security policies introduces risk that such transfers violate one or more domain security policies.

In such situations, information owners or stewards provide guidance at designated policy enforcement points between interconnected systems. Organizations consider mandating specific architectural solutions when required to enforce specific security policies. Enforcement includes: prohibiting information transfers between interconnected systems (i.e., allowing access only); employing hardware mechanisms to enforce one-way information flows; and implementing trustworthy regrading mechanisms to reassign security attributes and security labels.

<u>3.1.4</u>   **Separate the duties of individuals to reduce the risk of malevolent activity without collusion.**

DISCUSSION

Separation of duties addresses the potential for abuse of authorized privileges and helps to reduce the risk of malevolent activity without collusion. Separation of duties includes dividing mission functions and system support functions among different individuals or roles; conducting system support functions with different individuals (e.g., configuration management, quality assurance and testing, system management, programming, and network security); and ensuring that security personnel administering access control functions do not also administer audit functions. Because separation of duty violations can span systems and application domains, organizations consider the entirety of organizational systems and system components when developing policy on separation of duties.

<u>3.1.5</u>   **Employ the principle of least privilege, including for specific security functions and privileged accounts.**

DISCUSSION

Organizations employ the principle of least privilege for specific duties and authorized accesses for users and processes. The principle of least privilege is applied with the goal of authorized privileges no higher than necessary to accomplish required organizational missions or business functions. Organizations consider the creation of additional processes, roles, and system accounts as necessary, to achieve least privilege. Organizations also apply least privilege to the development, implementation, and operation of organizational systems. Security functions include establishing system accounts, setting events to be logged, setting intrusion detection parameters, and configuring access authorizations (i.e., permissions, privileges).

Privileged accounts, including super user accounts, are typically described as system administrator for various types of commercial off-the-shelf operating systems. Restricting privileged accounts to specific personnel or roles prevents day-to-day users from having access to privileged information or functions. Organizations may differentiate in the application of this requirement between allowed privileges for local accounts and for domain accounts provided organizations retain the ability to control system configurations for key security parameters and as otherwise necessary to sufficiently mitigate risk.

<u>3.1.6</u>   **Use non-privileged accounts or roles when accessing nonsecurity functions.**

DISCUSSION

This requirement limits exposure when operating from within privileged accounts or roles. The inclusion of roles addresses situations where organizations implement access control policies such as role-based access control and where a change of role provides the same degree of assurance in the change of access authorizations for the user and all processes acting on behalf of the user as would be provided by a change between a privileged and non-privileged account.

<u>3.1.7</u>   **Prevent non-privileged users from executing privileged functions and capture the execution of such functions in audit logs.**

DISCUSSION

Privileged functions include establishing system accounts, performing system integrity checks, conducting patching operations, or administering cryptographic key management activities. Non-privileged users are individuals that do not possess appropriate authorizations. Circumventing intrusion detection and prevention mechanisms or malicious code protection mechanisms are examples of privileged functions that require protection from non-privileged users. Note that this requirement represents a condition to be achieved by the definition of authorized privileges in 3.1.2.

Misuse of privileged functions, either intentionally or unintentionally by authorized users, or by unauthorized external entities that have compromised system accounts, is a serious and ongoing concern and can have significant adverse impacts on organizations. Logging the use of privileged functions is one way to detect such misuse, and in doing so, help mitigate the risk from insider threats and the advanced persistent threat.

3.1.8   Limit unsuccessful logon attempts.

DISCUSSION

This requirement applies regardless of whether the logon occurs via a local or network connection. Due to the potential for denial of service, automatic lockouts initiated by systems are, in most cases, temporary and automatically release after a predetermined period established by the organization (i.e., a delay algorithm). If a delay algorithm is selected, organizations may employ different algorithms for different system components based on the capabilities of the respective components. Responses to unsuccessful logon attempts may be implemented at the operating system and application levels.

3.1.9   Provide privacy and security notices consistent with applicable CUI rules.

DISCUSSION

System use notifications can be implemented using messages or warning banners displayed before individuals log in to organizational systems. System use notifications are used only for access via logon interfaces with human users and are not required when such human interfaces do not exist. Based on a risk assessment, organizations consider whether a secondary system use notification is needed to access applications or other system resources after the initial network logon. Where necessary, posters or other printed materials may be used in lieu of an automated system banner. Organizations consult with the Office of General Counsel for legal review and approval of warning banner content.

3.1.10   Use session lock with pattern-hiding displays to prevent access and viewing of data after a period of inactivity.

DISCUSSION

Session locks are temporary actions taken when users stop work and move away from the immediate vicinity of the system but do not want to log out because of the temporary nature of their absences. Session locks are implemented where session activities can be determined, typically at the operating system level (but can also be at the application level). Session locks are not an acceptable substitute for logging out of the system, for example, if organizations require users to log out at the end of the workday.

Pattern-hiding displays can include static or dynamic images, for example, patterns used with screen savers, photographic images, solid colors, clock, battery life indicator, or a blank screen, with the additional caveat that none of the images convey controlled unclassified information.

3.1.11   **Terminate (automatically) a user session after a defined condition.**

DISCUSSION

This requirement addresses the termination of user-initiated logical sessions in contrast to the termination of network connections that are associated with communications sessions (i.e., disconnecting from the network). A logical session (for local, network, and remote access) is initiated whenever a user (or process acting on behalf of a user) accesses an organizational system. Such user sessions can be terminated (and thus terminate user access) without terminating network sessions. Session termination terminates all processes associated with a user's logical session except those processes that are specifically created by the user (i.e., session owner) to continue after the session is terminated. Conditions or trigger events requiring automatic session termination can include organization-defined periods of user inactivity, targeted responses to certain types of incidents, and time-of-day restrictions on system use.

3.1.12   **Monitor and control remote access sessions.**

DISCUSSION

Remote access is access to organizational systems by users (or processes acting on behalf of users) communicating through external networks (e.g., the Internet). Remote access methods include dial-up, broadband, and wireless. Organizations often employ encrypted virtual private networks (VPNs) to enhance confidentiality over remote connections. The use of encrypted VPNs does not make the access non-remote; however, the use of VPNs, when adequately provisioned with appropriate control (e.g., employing encryption techniques for confidentiality protection), may provide sufficient assurance to the organization that it can effectively treat such connections as internal networks. VPNs with encrypted tunnels can affect the capability to adequately monitor network communications traffic for malicious code.

Automated monitoring and control of remote access sessions allows organizations to detect cyber-attacks and help to ensure ongoing compliance with remote access policies by auditing connection activities of remote users on a variety of system components (e.g., servers, workstations, notebook computers, smart phones, and tablets).

[SP 800-46], [SP 800-77], and [SP 800-113] provide guidance on secure remote access and virtual private networks.

3.1.13   **Employ cryptographic mechanisms to protect the confidentiality of remote access sessions.**

DISCUSSION

Cryptographic standards include FIPS-validated cryptography and NSA-approved cryptography. See [NIST CRYPTO]; [NIST CAVP]; [NIST CMVP]; NSA Cryptographic Standards.

3.1.14   **Route remote access via managed access control points.**

DISCUSSION

Routing remote access through managed access control points enhances explicit, organizational control over such connections, reducing the susceptibility to unauthorized access to organizational systems resulting in the unauthorized disclosure of CUI.

3.1.15   **Authorize remote execution of privileged commands and remote access to security-relevant information.**

DISCUSSION

A privileged command is a human-initiated (interactively or via a process operating on behalf of the human) command executed on a system involving the control, monitoring, or administration of the system including security functions and associated security-relevant information. Security-relevant information is any information within the system that can potentially impact the operation of security functions or the provision of security services in a manner that could result in failure to enforce the system security policy or maintain isolation of code and data. Privileged commands give individuals the ability to execute sensitive, security-critical, or security-relevant system functions. Controlling such access from remote locations helps to ensure that unauthorized individuals are not able to execute such commands freely with the potential to do serious or catastrophic damage to organizational systems. Note that the ability to affect the integrity of the system is considered security-relevant as that could enable the means to by-pass security functions although not directly impacting the function itself.

3.1.16 Authorize wireless access prior to allowing such connections.

DISCUSSION

Establishing usage restrictions and configuration/connection requirements for wireless access to the system provides criteria for organizations to support wireless access authorization decisions. Such restrictions and requirements reduce the susceptibility to unauthorized access to the system through wireless technologies. Wireless networks use authentication protocols which provide credential protection and mutual authentication.

[SP 800-97] provide guidance on secure wireless networks.

3.1.17 Protect wireless access using authentication and encryption.

DISCUSSION

Organizations authenticate individuals and devices to help protect wireless access to the system. Special attention is given to the wide variety of devices that are part of the Internet of Things with potential wireless access to organizational systems. See [NIST CRYPTO].

3.1.18 Control connection of mobile devices.

DISCUSSION

A mobile device is a computing device that has a small form factor such that it can easily be carried by a single individual; is designed to operate without a physical connection (e.g., wirelessly transmit or receive information); possesses local, non-removable or removable data storage; and includes a self-contained power source. Mobile devices may also include voice communication capabilities, on-board sensors that allow the device to capture information, or built-in features for synchronizing local data with remote locations. Examples of mobile devices include smart phones, e-readers, and tablets.

Due to the large variety of mobile devices with different technical characteristics and capabilities, organizational restrictions may vary for the different types of devices. Usage restrictions and implementation guidance for mobile devices include: device identification and authentication; configuration management; implementation of mandatory protective software (e.g., malicious code detection, firewall); scanning devices for malicious code; updating virus protection software; scanning for critical software updates and patches; conducting primary operating system (and possibly other resident software) integrity checks; and disabling unnecessary hardware (e.g., wireless, infrared). The need to provide adequate security for mobile devices goes beyond this requirement. Many controls for mobile devices are reflected in other CUI security requirements.

[SP 800-124] provides guidance on mobile device security.

3.1.19   **Encrypt CUI on mobile devices and mobile computing platforms.**[23]

DISCUSSION

Organizations can employ full-device encryption or container-based encryption to protect the confidentiality of CUI on mobile devices and computing platforms. Container-based encryption provides a more fine-grained approach to the encryption of data and information including encrypting selected data structures such as files, records, or fields. Protecting cryptographic keys is an essential element of any encryption solution. See [NIST CRYPTO].

3.1.20   **Verify and control/limit connections to and use of external systems.**

DISCUSSION

External systems are systems or components of systems for which organizations typically have no direct supervision and authority over the application of security requirements and controls or the determination of the effectiveness of implemented controls on those systems. External systems include personally owned systems, components, or devices and privately-owned computing and communications devices resident in commercial or public facilities. This requirement also addresses the use of external systems for the processing, storage, or transmission of CUI, including accessing cloud services (e.g., infrastructure as a service, platform as a service, or software as a service) from organizational systems.

Organizations establish terms and conditions for the use of external systems in accordance with organizational security policies and procedures. Terms and conditions address as a minimum, the types of applications that can be accessed on organizational systems from external systems. If terms and conditions with the owners of external systems cannot be established, organizations may impose restrictions on organizational personnel using those external systems.

This requirement recognizes that there are circumstances where individuals using external systems (e.g., contractors, coalition partners) need to access organizational systems. In those situations, organizations need confidence that the external systems contain the necessary controls so as not to compromise, damage, or otherwise harm organizational systems. Verification that the required controls have been effectively implemented can be achieved by third-party, independent assessments, attestations, or other means, depending on the assurance or confidence level required by organizations.

Note that while "external" typically refers to outside of the organization's direct supervision and authority, that is not always the case. Regarding the protection of CUI across an organization, the organization may have systems that process CUI and others that do not. And among the systems that process CUI there are likely access restrictions for CUI that apply between systems. Therefore, from the perspective of a given system, other systems within the organization may be considered "external" to that system.

3.1.21   **Limit use of portable storage devices on external systems.**

DISCUSSION

Limits on the use of organization-controlled portable storage devices in external systems include complete prohibition of the use of such devices or restrictions on how the devices may be used and under what conditions the devices may be used. Note that while "external" typically refers to outside of the organization's direct supervision and authority, that is not always the case. Regarding the protection of CUI across an organization, the organization may have systems that process CUI and others that do not. Among the systems that process CUI there are likely access

---

[23] Mobile devices and computing platforms include, for example, smartphones, tablets, and notebook computers.

restrictions for CUI that apply between systems. Therefore, from the perspective of a given system, other systems within the organization may be considered "external" to that system.

3.1.22   **Control CUI posted or processed on publicly accessible systems.**

DISCUSSION

In accordance with laws, Executive Orders, directives, policies, regulations, or standards, the public is not authorized access to nonpublic information (e.g., information protected under the Privacy Act, CUI, and proprietary information). This requirement addresses systems that are controlled by the organization and accessible to the public, typically without identification or authentication. Individuals authorized to post CUI onto publicly accessible systems are designated. The content of information is reviewed prior to posting onto publicly accessible systems to ensure that nonpublic information is not included.

3.2 AWARENESS AND TRAINING

Basic Security Requirements

3.2.1   **Ensure that managers, systems administrators, and users of organizational systems are made aware of the security risks associated with their activities and of the applicable policies, standards, and procedures related to the security of those systems.**

DISCUSSION

Organizations determine the content and frequency of security awareness training and security awareness techniques based on the specific organizational requirements and the systems to which personnel have authorized access. The content includes a basic understanding of the need for information security and user actions to maintain security and to respond to suspected security incidents. The content also addresses awareness of the need for operations security. Security awareness techniques include: formal training; offering supplies inscribed with security reminders; generating email advisories or notices from organizational officials; displaying logon screen messages; displaying security awareness posters; and conducting information security awareness events.

[SP 800-50] provides guidance on security awareness and training programs.

3.2.2   **Ensure that personnel are trained to carry out their assigned information security-related duties and responsibilities.**

DISCUSSION

Organizations determine the content and frequency of security training based on the assigned duties, roles, and responsibilities of individuals and the security requirements of organizations and the systems to which personnel have authorized access. In addition, organizations provide system developers, enterprise architects, security architects, acquisition/procurement officials, software developers, system developers, systems integrators, system/network administrators, personnel conducting configuration management and auditing activities, personnel performing independent verification and validation, security assessors, and other personnel having access to system-level software, security-related technical training specifically tailored for their assigned duties.

Comprehensive role-based training addresses management, operational, and technical roles and responsibilities covering physical, personnel, and technical controls. Such training can include policies, procedures, tools, and artifacts for the security roles defined. Organizations also provide the training necessary for individuals to carry out their responsibilities related to operations and supply chain security within the context of organizational information security programs.

[SP 800-181] provides guidance on role-based information security training in the workplace. [SP 800-161] provides guidance on supply chain risk management.

Derived Security Requirements

3.2.3   **Provide security awareness training on recognizing and reporting potential indicators of insider threat.**

DISCUSSION

Potential indicators and possible precursors of insider threat include behaviors such as: inordinate, long-term job dissatisfaction; attempts to gain access to information that is not required for job performance; unexplained access to financial resources; bullying or sexual harassment of fellow employees; workplace violence; and other serious violations of the policies, procedures, directives, rules, or practices of organizations. Security awareness training includes how to communicate employee and management concerns regarding potential indicators of insider threat through appropriate organizational channels in accordance with established organizational policies and procedures. Organizations may consider tailoring insider threat awareness topics to the role (e.g., training for managers may be focused on specific changes in behavior of team members, while training for employees may be focused on more general observations).

3.3 AUDIT AND ACCOUNTABILITY

Basic Security Requirements

3.3.1   **Create and retain system audit logs and records to the extent needed to enable the monitoring, analysis, investigation, and reporting of unlawful or unauthorized system activity.**

DISCUSSION

An event is any observable occurrence in a system, which includes unlawful or unauthorized system activity. Organizations identify event types for which a logging functionality is needed as those events which are significant and relevant to the security of systems and the environments in which those systems operate to meet specific and ongoing auditing needs. Event types can include password changes, failed logons or failed accesses related to systems, administrative privilege usage, or third-party credential usage. In determining event types that require logging, organizations consider the monitoring and auditing appropriate for each of the CUI security requirements. Monitoring and auditing requirements can be balanced with other system needs. For example, organizations may determine that systems must have the capability to log every file access both successful and unsuccessful, but not activate that capability except for specific circumstances due to the potential burden on system performance.

Audit records can be generated at various levels of abstraction, including at the packet level as information traverses the network. Selecting the appropriate level of abstraction is a critical aspect of an audit logging capability and can facilitate the identification of root causes to problems. Organizations consider in the definition of event types, the logging necessary to cover related events such as the steps in distributed, transaction-based processes (e.g., processes that are distributed across multiple organizations) and actions that occur in service-oriented or cloud-based architectures.

Audit record content that may be necessary to satisfy this requirement includes time stamps, source and destination addresses, user or process identifiers, event descriptions, success or fail indications, filenames involved, and access control or flow control rules invoked. Event outcomes can include indicators of event success or failure and event-specific results (e.g., the security state of the system after the event occurred).

Detailed information that organizations may consider in audit records includes full text recording of privileged commands or the individual identities of group account users. Organizations consider limiting the additional audit log information to only that information explicitly needed for specific audit requirements. This facilitates the use of audit trails and audit logs by not including information that could potentially be misleading or could make it more difficult to locate information of interest. Audit logs are reviewed and analyzed as often as needed to provide important information to organizations to facilitate risk-based decision making.

[SP 800-92] provides guidance on security log management.

3.3.2   **Ensure that the actions of individual system users can be uniquely traced to those users, so they can be held accountable for their actions.**

DISCUSSION

This requirement ensures that the contents of the audit record include the information needed to link the audit event to the actions of an individual to the extent feasible. Organizations consider logging for traceability including results from monitoring of account usage, remote access, wireless connectivity, mobile device connection, communications at system boundaries, configuration settings, physical access, nonlocal maintenance, use of maintenance tools, temperature and humidity, equipment delivery and removal, system component inventory, use of mobile code, and use of VoIP.

Derived Security Requirements

3.3.3   **Review and update logged events.**

DISCUSSION

The intent of this requirement is to periodically re-evaluate which logged events will continue to be included in the list of events to be logged. The event types that are logged by organizations may change over time. Reviewing and updating the set of logged event types periodically is necessary to ensure that the current set remains necessary and sufficient.

3.3.4   **Alert in the event of an audit logging process failure.**

DISCUSSION

Audit logging process failures include software and hardware errors, failures in the audit record capturing mechanisms, and audit record storage capacity being reached or exceeded. This requirement applies to each audit record data storage repository (i.e., distinct system component where audit records are stored), the total audit record storage capacity of organizations (i.e., all audit record data storage repositories combined), or both.

3.3.5   **Correlate audit record review, analysis, and reporting processes for investigation and response to indications of unlawful, unauthorized, suspicious, or unusual activity.**

DISCUSSION

Correlating audit record review, analysis, and reporting processes helps to ensure that they do not operate independently, but rather collectively. Regarding the assessment of a given organizational system, the requirement is agnostic as to whether this correlation is applied at the system level or at the organization level across all systems.

3.3.6   **Provide audit record reduction and report generation to support on-demand analysis and reporting.**

DISCUSSION

Audit record reduction is a process that manipulates collected audit information and organizes such information in a summary format that is more meaningful to analysts. Audit record reduction and report generation capabilities do not always emanate from the same system or organizational entities conducting auditing activities. Audit record reduction capability can include, for example, modern data mining techniques with advanced data filters to identify anomalous behavior in audit records. The report generation capability provided by the system can help generate customizable reports. Time ordering of audit records can be a significant issue if the granularity of the time stamp in the record is insufficient.

3.3.7   **Provide a system capability that compares and synchronizes internal system clocks with an authoritative source to generate time stamps for audit records.**

DISCUSSION

Internal system clocks are used to generate time stamps, which include date and time. Time is expressed in Coordinated Universal Time (UTC), a modern continuation of Greenwich Mean Time (GMT), or local time with an offset from UTC. The granularity of time measurements refers to the degree of synchronization between system clocks and reference clocks, for example, clocks synchronizing within hundreds of milliseconds or within tens of milliseconds. Organizations may define different time granularities for different system components. Time service can also be critical to other security capabilities such as access control and identification and authentication, depending on the nature of the mechanisms used to support those capabilities. This requirement provides uniformity of time stamps for systems with multiple system clocks and systems connected over a network. See [IETF 5905].

3.3.8   Protect audit information and audit logging tools from unauthorized access, modification, and deletion.

DISCUSSION

Audit information includes all information (e.g., audit records, audit log settings, and audit reports) needed to successfully audit system activity. Audit logging tools are those programs and devices used to conduct audit and logging activities. This requirement focuses on the technical protection of audit information and limits the ability to access and execute audit logging tools to authorized individuals. Physical protection of audit information is addressed by media protection and physical and environmental protection requirements.

3.3.9   Limit management of audit logging functionality to a subset of privileged users.

DISCUSSION

Individuals with privileged access to a system and who are also the subject of an audit by that system, may affect the reliability of audit information by inhibiting audit logging activities or modifying audit records. This requirement specifies that privileged access be further defined between audit-related privileges and other privileges, thus limiting the users with audit-related privileges.

3.4 CONFIGURATION MANAGEMENT

Basic Security Requirements

3.4.1   **Establish and maintain baseline configurations and inventories of organizational systems (including hardware, software, firmware, and documentation) throughout the respective system development life cycles.**

DISCUSSION

This requirement establishes and maintains baseline configurations for systems and system components including for system communications and connectivity. Baseline configurations are documented, formally reviewed, and agreed-upon sets of specifications for systems or configuration items within those systems. Baseline configurations serve as a basis for future builds, releases, and changes to systems. Baseline configurations include information about system components (e.g., standard software packages installed on workstations, notebook computers, servers, network components, or mobile devices; current version numbers and update and patch information on operating systems and applications; and configuration settings and parameters), network topology, and the logical placement of those components within the system architecture. Baseline configurations of systems also reflect the current enterprise architecture. Maintaining effective baseline configurations requires creating new baselines as organizational systems change over time. Baseline configuration maintenance includes reviewing and updating the baseline configuration when changes are made based on security risks and deviations from the established baseline configuration

Organizations can implement centralized system component inventories that include components from multiple organizational systems. In such situations, organizations ensure that the resulting inventories include system-specific information required for proper component accountability (e.g., system association, system owner). Information deemed necessary for effective accountability of system components includes hardware inventory specifications, software license information, software version numbers, component owners, and for networked components or devices, machine names and network addresses. Inventory specifications include manufacturer, device type, model, serial number, and physical location.

[SP 800-128] provides guidance on security-focused configuration management.

3.4.2   **Establish and enforce security configuration settings for information technology products employed in organizational systems.**

DISCUSSION

Configuration settings are the set of parameters that can be changed in hardware, software, or firmware components of the system that affect the security posture or functionality of the system. Information technology products for which security-related configuration settings can be defined include mainframe computers, servers, workstations, input and output devices (e.g., scanners, copiers, and printers), network components (e.g., firewalls, routers, gateways, voice and data switches, wireless access points, network appliances, sensors), operating systems, middleware, and applications.

Security parameters are those parameters impacting the security state of systems including the parameters required to satisfy other security requirements. Security parameters include: registry settings; account, file, directory permission settings; and settings for functions, ports, protocols, and remote connections. Organizations establish organization-wide configuration settings and subsequently derive specific configuration settings for systems. The established settings become part of the systems configuration baseline.

Common secure configurations (also referred to as security configuration checklists, lockdown and hardening guides, security reference guides, security technical implementation guides) provide recognized, standardized, and established benchmarks that stipulate secure configuration settings for specific information technology platforms/products and instructions for configuring those system components to meet operational requirements. Common secure configurations can be developed by a variety of organizations including information technology product developers, manufacturers, vendors, consortia, academia, industry, federal agencies, and other organizations in the public and private sectors.

[SP 800-70] and [SP 800-128] provide guidance on security configuration settings.

Derived Security Requirements

3.4.3   **Track, review, approve or disapprove, and log changes to organizational systems.**

DISCUSSION

Tracking, reviewing, approving/disapproving, and logging changes is called configuration change control. Configuration change control for organizational systems involves the systematic proposal, justification, implementation, testing, review, and disposition of changes to the systems, including system upgrades and modifications. Configuration change control includes changes to baseline configurations for components and configuration items of systems, changes to configuration settings for information technology products (e.g., operating systems, applications, firewalls, routers, and mobile devices), unscheduled and unauthorized changes, and changes to remediate vulnerabilities.

Processes for managing configuration changes to systems include Configuration Control Boards or Change Advisory Boards that review and approve proposed changes to systems. For new development systems or systems undergoing major upgrades, organizations consider including representatives from development organizations on the Configuration Control Boards or Change Advisory Boards. Audit logs of changes include activities before and after changes are made to organizational systems and the activities required to implement such changes.

[SP 800-128] provides guidance on configuration change control.

3.4.4   **Analyze the security impact of changes prior to implementation.**

DISCUSSION

Organizational personnel with information security responsibilities (e.g., system administrators, system security officers, system security managers, and systems security engineers) conduct security impact analyses. Individuals conducting security impact analyses possess the necessary skills and technical expertise to analyze the changes to systems and the associated security ramifications. Security impact analysis may include reviewing security plans to understand security requirements and reviewing system design documentation to understand the implementation of controls and how specific changes might affect the controls. Security impact analyses may also include risk assessments to better understand the impact of the changes and to determine if additional controls are required.

[SP 800-128] provides guidance on configuration change control and security impact analysis.

3.4.5   **Define, document, approve, and enforce physical and logical access restrictions associated with changes to organizational systems.**

DISCUSSION

Any changes to the hardware, software, or firmware components of systems can potentially have significant effects on the overall security of the systems. Therefore, organizations permit only qualified and authorized individuals to access systems for purposes of initiating changes, including upgrades and modifications. Access restrictions for change also include software libraries.

Access restrictions include physical and logical access control requirements, workflow automation, media libraries, abstract layers (e.g., changes implemented into external interfaces rather than directly into systems), and change windows (e.g., changes occur only during certain specified times). In addition to security concerns, commonly-accepted due diligence for configuration management includes access restrictions as an essential part in ensuring the ability to effectively manage the configuration.

[SP 800-128] provides guidance on configuration change control.

3.4.6   **Employ the principle of least functionality by configuring organizational systems to provide only essential capabilities.**

DISCUSSION

Systems can provide a wide variety of functions and services. Some of the functions and services routinely provided by default, may not be necessary to support essential organizational missions, functions, or operations. It is sometimes convenient to provide multiple services from single system components. However, doing so increases risk over limiting the services provided by any one component. Where feasible, organizations limit component functionality to a single function per component.

Organizations review functions and services provided by systems or components of systems, to determine which functions and services are candidates for elimination. Organizations disable unused or unnecessary physical and logical ports and protocols to prevent unauthorized connection of devices, transfer of information, and tunneling. Organizations can utilize network scanning tools, intrusion detection and prevention systems, and end-point protections such as firewalls and host-based intrusion detection systems to identify and prevent the use of prohibited functions, ports, protocols, and services.

3.4.7   **Restrict, disable, or prevent the use of nonessential programs, functions, ports, protocols, and services.**

DISCUSSION

Restricting the use of nonessential software (programs) includes restricting the roles allowed to approve program execution; prohibiting auto-execute; program blacklisting and whitelisting; or restricting the number of program instances executed at the same time. The organization makes a security-based determination which functions, ports, protocols, and/or services are restricted. Bluetooth, FTP, and peer-to-peer networking are examples of protocols organizations consider preventing the use of, restricting, or disabling.

3.4.8   **Apply deny-by-exception (blacklisting) policy to prevent the use of unauthorized software or deny-all, permit-by-exception (whitelisting) policy to allow the execution of authorized software.**

DISCUSSION

The process used to identify software programs that are not authorized to execute on systems is commonly referred to as blacklisting. The process used to identify software programs that are authorized to execute on systems is commonly referred to as whitelisting. Whitelisting is the stronger of the two policies for restricting software program execution. In addition to whitelisting, organizations consider verifying the integrity of whitelisted software programs using, for example, cryptographic checksums, digital signatures, or hash functions. Verification of whitelisted software can occur either prior to execution or at system startup.

[SP 800-167] provides guidance on application whitelisting.

3.4.9   Control and monitor user-installed software.

DISCUSSION

Users can install software in organizational systems if provided the necessary privileges. To maintain control over the software installed, organizations identify permitted and prohibited actions regarding software installation through policies. Permitted software installations include updates and security patches to existing software and applications from organization-approved "app stores." Prohibited software installations may include software with unknown or suspect pedigrees or software that organizations consider potentially malicious. The policies organizations select governing user-installed software may be organization-developed or provided by some external entity. Policy enforcement methods include procedural methods, automated methods, or both.

3.5 IDENTIFICATION AND AUTHENTICATION

Basic Security Requirements

3.5.1 **Identify system users, processes acting on behalf of users, and devices.**

    DISCUSSION

    Common device identifiers include media access control (MAC), Internet protocol (IP) addresses, or device-unique token identifiers. Management of individual identifiers is not applicable to shared system accounts. Typically, individual identifiers are the user names associated with the system accounts assigned to those individuals. Organizations may require unique identification of individuals in group accounts or for detailed accountability of individual activity. In addition, this requirement addresses individual identifiers that are not necessarily associated with system accounts. Organizational devices requiring identification may be defined by type, by device, or by a combination of type/device.

    [SP 800-63-3] provides guidance on digital identities.

3.5.2 **Authenticate (or verify) the identities of users, processes, or devices, as a prerequisite to allowing access to organizational systems.**

    DISCUSSION

    Individual authenticators include the following: passwords, key cards, cryptographic devices, and one-time password devices. Initial authenticator content is the actual content of the authenticator, for example, the initial password. In contrast, the requirements about authenticator content include the minimum password length. Developers ship system components with factory default authentication credentials to allow for initial installation and configuration. Default authentication credentials are often well known, easily discoverable, and present a significant security risk.

    Systems support authenticator management by organization-defined settings and restrictions for various authenticator characteristics including minimum password length, validation time window for time synchronous one-time tokens, and number of allowed rejections during the verification stage of biometric authentication. Authenticator management includes issuing and revoking, when no longer needed, authenticators for temporary access such as that required for remote maintenance. Device authenticators include certificates and passwords.

    [SP 800-63-3] provides guidance on digital identities.

Derived Security Requirements

3.5.3 **Use multifactor authentication for local and network access to privileged accounts and for network access to non-privileged accounts.** [24] [25]

---

[24] *Multifactor authentication* requires two or more different factors to achieve authentication. The factors include: something you know (e.g., password/PIN); something you have (e.g., cryptographic identification device, token); or something you are (e.g., biometric). The requirement for multifactor authentication should not be interpreted as requiring federal Personal Identity Verification (PIV) card or Department of Defense Common Access Card (CAC)-like solutions. A variety of multifactor solutions (including those with replay resistance) using tokens and biometrics are commercially available. Such solutions may employ hard tokens (e.g., smartcards, key fobs, or dongles) or soft tokens to store user credentials.

[25] *Local access* is any access to a system by a user (or process acting on behalf of a user) communicating through a direct connection without the use of a network. *Network access* is any access to a system by a user (or a process acting on behalf of a user) communicating through a network (e.g., local area network, wide area network, Internet).

DISCUSSION

Multifactor authentication requires the use of two or more different factors to authenticate. The factors are defined as something you know (e.g., password, personal identification number [PIN]); something you have (e.g., cryptographic identification device, token); or something you are (e.g., biometric). Multifactor authentication solutions that feature physical authenticators include hardware authenticators providing time-based or challenge-response authenticators and smart cards. In addition to authenticating users at the system level (i.e., at logon), organizations may also employ authentication mechanisms at the application level, when necessary, to provide increased information security.

Access to organizational systems is defined as local access or network access. Local access is any access to organizational systems by users (or processes acting on behalf of users) where such access is obtained by direct connections without the use of networks. Network access is access to systems by users (or processes acting on behalf of users) where such access is obtained through network connections (i.e., nonlocal accesses). Remote access is a type of network access that involves communication through external networks. The use of encrypted virtual private networks for connections between organization-controlled and non-organization controlled endpoints may be treated as internal networks with regard to protecting the confidentiality of information.

[SP 800-63-3] provides guidance on digital identities.

3.5.4   **Employ replay-resistant authentication mechanisms for network access to privileged and non-privileged accounts.**

DISCUSSION

Authentication processes resist replay attacks if it is impractical to successfully authenticate by recording or replaying previous authentication messages. Replay-resistant techniques include protocols that use nonces or challenges such as time synchronous or challenge-response one-time authenticators.

[SP 800-63-3] provides guidance on digital identities.

3.5.5   **Prevent reuse of identifiers for a defined period.**

DISCUSSION

Identifiers are provided for users, processes acting on behalf of users, or devices (3.5.1). Preventing reuse of identifiers implies preventing the assignment of previously used individual, group, role, or device identifiers to different individuals, groups, roles, or devices.

3.5.6   **Disable identifiers after a defined period of inactivity.**

DISCUSSION

Inactive identifiers pose a risk to organizational information because attackers may exploit an inactive identifier to gain undetected access to organizational devices. The owners of the inactive accounts may not notice if unauthorized access to the account has been obtained.

3.5.7   **Enforce a minimum password complexity and change of characters when new passwords are created.**

DISCUSSION

This requirement applies to single-factor authentication of individuals using passwords as individual or group authenticators, and in a similar manner, when passwords are used as part of multifactor authenticators. The number of changed characters refers to the number of changes required with respect to the total number of positions in the current password. To mitigate certain brute force attacks against passwords, organizations may also consider salting passwords.

3.5.8   Prohibit password reuse for a specified number of generations.

DISCUSSION

Password lifetime restrictions do not apply to temporary passwords.

3.5.9   Allow temporary password use for system logons with an immediate change to a permanent password.

DISCUSSION

Changing temporary passwords to permanent passwords immediately after system logon ensures that the necessary strength of the authentication mechanism is implemented at the earliest opportunity, reducing the susceptibility to authenticator compromises.

3.5.10   Store and transmit only cryptographically-protected passwords.

DISCUSSION

Cryptographically-protected passwords use salted one-way cryptographic hashes of passwords. See [NIST CRYPTO].

3.5.11   Obscure feedback of authentication information.

DISCUSSION

The feedback from systems does not provide any information that would allow unauthorized individuals to compromise authentication mechanisms. For some types of systems or system components, for example, desktop or notebook computers with relatively large monitors, the threat (often referred to as shoulder surfing) may be significant. For other types of systems or components, for example, mobile devices with small displays, this threat may be less significant, and is balanced against the increased likelihood of typographic input errors due to the small keyboards. Therefore, the means for obscuring the authenticator feedback is selected accordingly. Obscuring authenticator feedback includes displaying asterisks when users type passwords into input devices or displaying feedback for a very limited time before fully obscuring it.

3.6 INCIDENT RESPONSE

Basic Security Requirements

3.6.1   **Establish an operational incident-handling capability for organizational systems that includes preparation, detection, analysis, containment, recovery, and user response activities.**

DISCUSSION

Organizations recognize that incident handling capability is dependent on the capabilities of organizational systems and the mission/business processes being supported by those systems. Organizations consider incident handling as part of the definition, design, and development of mission/business processes and systems. Incident-related information can be obtained from a variety of sources including audit monitoring, network monitoring, physical access monitoring, user and administrator reports, and reported supply chain events. Effective incident handling capability includes coordination among many organizational entities including mission/business owners, system owners, authorizing officials, human resources offices, physical and personnel security offices, legal departments, operations personnel, procurement offices, and the risk executive.

As part of user response activities, incident response training is provided by organizations and is linked directly to the assigned roles and responsibilities of organizational personnel to ensure that the appropriate content and level of detail is included in such training. For example, regular users may only need to know who to call or how to recognize an incident on the system; system administrators may require additional training on how to handle or remediate incidents; and incident responders may receive more specific training on forensics, reporting, system recovery, and restoration. Incident response training includes user training in the identification/reporting of suspicious activities from external and internal sources. User response activities also includes incident response assistance which may consist of help desk support, assistance groups, and access to forensics services or consumer redress services, when required.

[SP 800-61] provides guidance on incident handling. [SP 800-86] and [SP 800-101] provide guidance on integrating forensic techniques into incident response. [SP 800-161] provides guidance on supply chain risk management.

3.6.2   **Track, document, and report incidents to designated officials and/or authorities both internal and external to the organization.**

DISCUSSION

Tracking and documenting system security incidents includes maintaining records about each incident, the status of the incident, and other pertinent information necessary for forensics, evaluating incident details, trends, and handling. Incident information can be obtained from a variety of sources including incident reports, incident response teams, audit monitoring, network monitoring, physical access monitoring, and user/administrator reports.

Reporting incidents addresses specific incident reporting requirements within an organization and the formal incident reporting requirements for the organization. Suspected security incidents may also be reported and include the receipt of suspicious email communications that can potentially contain malicious code. The types of security incidents reported, the content and timeliness of the reports, and the designated reporting authorities reflect applicable laws, Executive Orders, directives, regulations, and policies.

[SP 800-61] provides guidance on incident handling.

Derived Security Requirements

3.6.3   **Test the organizational incident response capability.**

DISCUSSION

Organizations test incident response capabilities to determine the effectiveness of the capabilities and to identify potential weaknesses or deficiencies. Incident response testing includes the use of checklists, walk-through or tabletop exercises, simulations (both parallel and full interrupt), and comprehensive exercises. Incident response testing can also include a determination of the effects on organizational operations (e.g., reduction in mission capabilities), organizational assets, and individuals due to incident response.

[SP 800-84] provides guidance on testing programs for information technology capabilities.

3.7 MAINTENANCE

Basic Security Requirements

3.7.1   **Perform maintenance on organizational systems.**[26]

DISCUSSION

This requirement addresses the information security aspects of the system maintenance program and applies to all types of maintenance to any system component (including hardware, firmware, applications) conducted by any local or nonlocal entity. System maintenance also includes those components not directly associated with information processing and data or information retention such as scanners, copiers, and printers.

3.7.2   **Provide controls on the tools, techniques, mechanisms, and personnel used to conduct system maintenance.**

DISCUSSION

This requirement addresses security-related issues with maintenance tools that are not within the organizational system boundaries that process, store, or transmit CUI, but are used specifically for diagnostic and repair actions on those systems. Organizations have flexibility in determining the controls in place for maintenance tools, but can include approving, controlling, and monitoring the use of such tools. Maintenance tools are potential vehicles for transporting malicious code, either intentionally or unintentionally, into a facility and into organizational systems. Maintenance tools can include hardware, software, and firmware items, for example, hardware and software diagnostic test equipment and hardware and software packet sniffers.

Derived Security Requirements

3.7.3   **Ensure equipment removed for off-site maintenance is sanitized of any CUI.**

DISCUSSION

This requirement addresses the information security aspects of system maintenance that are performed off-site and applies to all types of maintenance to any system component (including applications) conducted by a local or nonlocal entity (e.g., in-contract, warranty, in- house, software maintenance agreement).

[SP 800-88] provides guidance on media sanitization.

3.7.4   **Check media containing diagnostic and test programs for malicious code before the media are used in organizational systems.**

DISCUSSION

If, upon inspection of media containing maintenance diagnostic and test programs, organizations determine that the media contain malicious code, the incident is handled consistent with incident handling policies and procedures.

3.7.5   **Require multifactor authentication to establish nonlocal maintenance sessions via external network connections and terminate such connections when nonlocal maintenance is complete.**

---

[26] In general, system maintenance requirements tend to support the security objective of *availability*. However, improper system maintenance or a failure to perform maintenance can result in the unauthorized disclosure of CUI, thus compromising *confidentiality* of that information.

DISCUSSION

Nonlocal maintenance and diagnostic activities are those activities conducted by individuals communicating through an external network. The authentication techniques employed in the establishment of these nonlocal maintenance and diagnostic sessions reflect the network access requirements in 3.5.3.

3.7.6   **Supervise the maintenance activities of maintenance personnel without required access authorization.**

DISCUSSION

This requirement applies to individuals who are performing hardware or software maintenance on organizational systems, while 3.10.1 addresses physical access for individuals whose maintenance duties place them within the physical protection perimeter of the systems (e.g., custodial staff, physical plant maintenance personnel). Individuals not previously identified as authorized maintenance personnel, such as information technology manufacturers, vendors, consultants, and systems integrators, may require privileged access to organizational systems, for example, when required to conduct maintenance activities with little or no notice. Organizations may choose to issue temporary credentials to these individuals based on organizational risk assessments. Temporary credentials may be for one-time use or for very limited time periods.

3.8 MEDIA PROTECTION

Basic Security Requirements

<u>3.8.1</u>   **Protect (i.e., physically control and securely store) system media containing CUI, both paper and digital.**

DISCUSSION

System media includes digital and non-digital media. Digital media includes diskettes, magnetic tapes, external and removable hard disk drives, flash drives, compact disks, and digital video disks. Non-digital media includes paper and microfilm. Protecting digital media includes limiting access to design specifications stored on compact disks or flash drives in the media library to the project leader and any individuals on the development team. Physically controlling system media includes conducting inventories, maintaining accountability for stored media, and ensuring procedures are in place to allow individuals to check out and return media to the media library. Secure storage includes a locked drawer, desk, or cabinet, or a controlled media library.

Access to CUI on system media can be limited by physically controlling such media, which includes conducting inventories, ensuring procedures are in place to allow individuals to check out and return media to the media library, and maintaining accountability for all stored media.

[SP 800-111] provides guidance on storage encryption technologies for end user devices.

<u>3.8.2</u>   **Limit access to CUI on system media to authorized users.**

DISCUSSION

Access can be limited by physically controlling system media and secure storage areas. Physically controlling system media includes conducting inventories, ensuring procedures are in place to allow individuals to check out and return system media to the media library, and maintaining accountability for all stored media. Secure storage includes a locked drawer, desk, or cabinet, or a controlled media library.

<u>3.8.3</u>   **Sanitize or destroy system media containing CUI before disposal or release for reuse.**

DISCUSSION

This requirement applies to all system media, digital and non-digital, subject to disposal or reuse. Examples include: digital media found in workstations, network components, scanners, copiers, printers, notebook computers, and mobile devices; and non-digital media such as paper and microfilm. The sanitization process removes information from the media such that the information cannot be retrieved or reconstructed. Sanitization techniques, including clearing, purging, cryptographic erase, and destruction, prevent the disclosure of information to unauthorized individuals when such media is released for reuse or disposal.

Organizations determine the appropriate sanitization methods, recognizing that destruction may be necessary when other methods cannot be applied to the media requiring sanitization. Organizations use discretion on the employment of sanitization techniques and procedures for media containing information that is in the public domain or publicly releasable or deemed to have no adverse impact on organizations or individuals if released for reuse or disposal. Sanitization of non-digital media includes destruction, removing CUI from documents, or redacting selected sections or words from a document by obscuring the redacted sections or words in a manner equivalent in effectiveness to removing the words or sections from the document. NARA policy and guidance control sanitization processes for controlled unclassified information.

[SP 800-88] provides guidance on media sanitization.

Derived Security Requirements

3.8.4   Mark media with necessary CUI markings and distribution limitations.[27]

DISCUSSION

The term security marking refers to the application or use of human-readable security attributes. System media includes digital and non-digital media. Marking of system media reflects applicable federal laws, Executive Orders, directives, policies, and regulations. See [NARA MARK].

3.8.5   Control access to media containing CUI and maintain accountability for media during transport outside of controlled areas.

DISCUSSION

Controlled areas are areas or spaces for which organizations provide physical or procedural controls to meet the requirements established for protecting systems and information. Controls to maintain accountability for media during transport include locked containers and cryptography. Cryptographic mechanisms can provide confidentiality and integrity protections depending upon the mechanisms used. Activities associated with transport include the actual transport as well as those activities such as releasing media for transport and ensuring that media enters the appropriate transport processes. For the actual transport, authorized transport and courier personnel may include individuals external to the organization. Maintaining accountability of media during transport includes restricting transport activities to authorized personnel and tracking and obtaining explicit records of transport activities as the media moves through the transportation system to prevent and detect loss, destruction, or tampering.

3.8.6   Implement cryptographic mechanisms to protect the confidentiality of CUI stored on digital media during transport unless otherwise protected by alternative physical safeguards.

DISCUSSION

This requirement applies to portable storage devices (e.g., USB memory sticks, digital video disks, compact disks, external or removable hard disk drives). See [NIST CRYPTO].

[SP 800-111] provides guidance on storage encryption technologies for end user devices.

3.8.7   Control the use of removable media on system components.

DISCUSSION

In contrast to requirement 3.8.1, which restricts user access to media, this requirement restricts the use of certain types of media on systems, for example, restricting or prohibiting the use of flash drives or external hard disk drives. Organizations can employ technical and nontechnical controls (e.g., policies, procedures, and rules of behavior) to control the use of system media. Organizations may control the use of portable storage devices, for example, by using physical cages on workstations to prohibit access to certain external ports, or disabling or removing the ability to insert, read, or write to such devices.

Organizations may also limit the use of portable storage devices to only approved devices including devices provided by the organization, devices provided by other approved organizations, and devices that are not personally owned. Finally, organizations may control the use of portable storage devices based on the type of device, prohibiting the use of writeable, portable devices, and implementing this restriction by disabling or removing the capability to write to such devices.

---

[27] The implementation of this requirement is per marking guidance in [32 CFR 2002] and [NARA CUI].

3.8.8   **Prohibit the use of portable storage devices when such devices have no identifiable owner.**

DISCUSSION

Requiring identifiable owners (e.g., individuals, organizations, or projects) for portable storage devices reduces the overall risk of using such technologies by allowing organizations to assign responsibility and accountability for addressing known vulnerabilities in the devices (e.g., insertion of malicious code).

3.8.9   **Protect the confidentiality of backup CUI at storage locations.**

DISCUSSION

Organizations can employ cryptographic mechanisms or alternative physical controls to protect the confidentiality of backup information at designated storage locations. Backed-up information containing CUI may include system-level information and user-level information. System-level information includes system-state information, operating system software, application software, and licenses. User-level information includes information other than system-level information.

3.9 PERSONNEL SECURITY

Basic Security Requirements

3.9.1   **Screen individuals prior to authorizing access to organizational systems containing CUI.**

DISCUSSION

Personnel security screening (vetting) activities involve the evaluation/assessment of individual's conduct, integrity, judgment, loyalty, reliability, and stability (i.e., the trustworthiness of the individual) prior to authorizing access to organizational systems containing CUI. The screening activities reflect applicable federal laws, Executive Orders, directives, policies, regulations, and specific criteria established for the level of access required for assigned positions.

3.9.2   **Ensure that organizational systems containing CUI are protected during and after personnel actions such as terminations and transfers.**

DISCUSSION

Protecting CUI during and after personnel actions may include returning system-related property and conducting exit interviews. System-related property includes hardware authentication tokens, identification cards, system administration technical manuals, keys, and building passes. Exit interviews ensure that individuals who have been terminated understand the security constraints imposed by being former employees and that proper accountability is achieved for system-related property. Security topics of interest at exit interviews can include reminding terminated individuals of nondisclosure agreements and potential limitations on future employment. Exit interviews may not be possible for some terminated individuals, for example, in cases related to job abandonment, illnesses, and non-availability of supervisors. For termination actions, timely execution is essential for individuals terminated for cause. In certain situations, organizations consider disabling the system accounts of individuals that are being terminated prior to the individuals being notified.

This requirement applies to reassignments or transfers of individuals when the personnel action is permanent or of such extended durations as to require protection. Organizations define the CUI protections appropriate for the types of reassignments or transfers, whether permanent or extended. Protections that may be required for transfers or reassignments to other positions within organizations include returning old and issuing new keys, identification cards, and building passes; changing system access authorizations (i.e., privileges); closing system accounts and establishing new accounts; and providing for access to official records to which individuals had access at previous work locations and in previous system accounts.

Derived Security Requirements

None.

3.10 PHYSICAL PROTECTION

Basic Security Requirements

3.10.1   **Limit physical access to organizational systems, equipment, and the respective operating environments to authorized individuals.**

DISCUSSION

This requirement applies to employees, individuals with permanent physical access authorization credentials, and visitors. Authorized individuals have credentials that include badges, identification cards, and smart cards. Organizations determine the strength of authorization credentials needed consistent with applicable laws, directives, policies, regulations, standards, procedures, and guidelines. This requirement applies only to areas within facilities that have not been designated as publicly accessible.

Limiting physical access to equipment may include placing equipment in locked rooms or other secured areas and allowing access to authorized individuals only; and placing equipment in locations that can be monitored by organizational personnel. Computing devices, external disk drives, networking devices, monitors, printers, copiers, scanners, facsimile machines, and audio devices are examples of equipment.

3.10.2   **Protect and monitor the physical facility and support infrastructure for organizational systems.**

DISCUSSION

Monitoring of physical access includes publicly accessible areas within organizational facilities. This can be accomplished, for example, by the employment of guards; the use of sensor devices; or the use of video surveillance equipment such as cameras. Examples of support infrastructure include system distribution, transmission, and power lines. Security controls applied to the support infrastructure prevent accidental damage, disruption, and physical tampering. Such controls may also be necessary to prevent eavesdropping or modification of unencrypted transmissions. Physical access controls to support infrastructure include locked wiring closets; disconnected or locked spare jacks; protection of cabling by conduit or cable trays; and wiretapping sensors.

Derived Security Requirements

3.10.3   **Escort visitors and monitor visitor activity.**

DISCUSSION

Individuals with permanent physical access authorization credentials are not considered visitors. Audit logs can be used to monitor visitor activity.

3.10.4   **Maintain audit logs of physical access.**

DISCUSSION

Organizations have flexibility in the types of audit logs employed. Audit logs can be procedural (e.g., a written log of individuals accessing the facility), automated (e.g., capturing ID provided by a PIV card), or some combination thereof. Physical access points can include facility access points, interior access points to systems or system components requiring supplemental access controls, or both. System components (e.g., workstations, notebook computers) may be in areas designated as publicly accessible with organizations safeguarding access to such devices.

3.10.5   **Control and manage physical access devices.**

DISCUSSION

Physical access devices include keys, locks, combinations, and card readers.

3.10.6   **Enforce safeguarding measures for CUI at alternate work sites.**

DISCUSSION

Alternate work sites may include government facilities or the private residences of employees. Organizations may define different security requirements for specific alternate work sites or types of sites depending on the work-related activities conducted at those sites.

[SP 800-46] and [SP 800-114] provide guidance on enterprise and user security when teleworking.

3.11 RISK ASSESSMENT

Basic Security Requirements

3.11.1   **Periodically assess the risk to organizational operations (including mission, functions, image, or reputation), organizational assets, and individuals, resulting from the operation of organizational systems and the associated processing, storage, or transmission of CUI.**

DISCUSSION

Clearly defined system boundaries are a prerequisite for effective risk assessments. Such risk assessments consider threats, vulnerabilities, likelihood, and impact to organizational operations, organizational assets, and individuals based on the operation and use of organizational systems. Risk assessments also consider risk from external parties (e.g., service providers, contractors operating systems on behalf of the organization, individuals accessing organizational systems, outsourcing entities). Risk assessments, either formal or informal, can be conducted at the organization level, the mission or business process level, or the system level, and at any phase in the system development life cycle.

[SP 800-30] provides guidance on conducting risk assessments.

Derived Security Requirements

3.11.2   **Scan for vulnerabilities in organizational systems and applications periodically and when new vulnerabilities affecting those systems and applications are identified.**

DISCUSSION

Alternate work sites Organizations determine the required vulnerability scanning for all system components, ensuring that potential sources of vulnerabilities such as networked printers, scanners, and copiers are not overlooked. The vulnerabilities to be scanned are readily updated as new vulnerabilities are discovered, announced, and scanning methods developed. This process ensures that potential vulnerabilities in the system are identified and addressed as quickly as possible. Vulnerability analyses for custom software applications may require additional approaches such as static analysis, dynamic analysis, binary analysis, or a hybrid of the three approaches. Organizations can employ these analysis approaches in source code reviews and in a variety of tools (e.g., static analysis tools, web-based application scanners, binary analyzers) and in source code reviews. Vulnerability scanning includes: scanning for patch levels; scanning for functions, ports, protocols, and services that should not be accessible to users or devices; and scanning for improperly configured or incorrectly operating information flow control mechanisms.

To facilitate interoperability, organizations consider using products that are Security Content Automated Protocol (SCAP)-validated, scanning tools that express vulnerabilities in the Common Vulnerabilities and Exposures (CVE) naming convention, and that employ the Open Vulnerability Assessment Language (OVAL) to determine the presence of system vulnerabilities. Sources for vulnerability information include the Common Weakness Enumeration (CWE) listing and the National Vulnerability Database (NVD).

Security assessments, such as red team exercises, provide additional sources of potential vulnerabilities for which to scan. Organizations also consider using scanning tools that express vulnerability impact by the Common Vulnerability Scoring System (CVSS). In certain situations, the nature of the vulnerability scanning may be more intrusive or the system component that is the subject of the scanning may contain highly sensitive information. Privileged access authorization to selected system components facilitates thorough vulnerability scanning and protects the sensitive nature of such scanning.

[SP 800-40] provides guidance on vulnerability management.

<u>3.11.3</u>   **Remediate vulnerabilities in accordance with risk assessments.**

DISCUSSION

Vulnerabilities discovered, for example, via the scanning conducted in response to <u>3.11.2</u>, are remediated with consideration of the related assessment of risk. The consideration of risk influences the prioritization of remediation efforts and the level of effort to be expended in the remediation for specific vulnerabilities.

3.12 SECURITY ASSESSMENT

Basic Security Requirements

<u>3.12.1</u> **Periodically assess the security controls in organizational systems to determine if the controls are effective in their application.**

DISCUSSION

Organizations assess security controls in organizational systems and the environments in which those systems operate as part of the system development life cycle. Security controls are the safeguards or countermeasures organizations implement to satisfy security requirements. By assessing the implemented security controls, organizations determine if the security safeguards or countermeasures are in place and operating as intended. Security control assessments ensure that information security is built into organizational systems; identify weaknesses and deficiencies early in the development process; provide essential information needed to make risk-based decisions; and ensure compliance to vulnerability mitigation procedures. Assessments are conducted on the implemented security controls as documented in system security plans.

Security assessment reports document assessment results in sufficient detail as deemed necessary by organizations, to determine the accuracy and completeness of the reports and whether the security controls are implemented correctly, operating as intended, and producing the desired outcome with respect to meeting security requirements. Security assessment results are provided to the individuals or roles appropriate for the types of assessments being conducted.

Organizations ensure that security assessment results are current, relevant to the determination of security control effectiveness, and obtained with the appropriate level of assessor independence. Organizations can choose to use other types of assessment activities such as vulnerability scanning and system monitoring to maintain the security posture of systems during the system life cycle.

[SP 800-53] provides guidance on security and privacy controls for systems and organizations. [SP 800-53A] provides guidance on developing security assessment plans and conducting assessments.

<u>3.12.2</u> **Develop and implement plans of action designed to correct deficiencies and reduce or eliminate vulnerabilities in organizational systems.**

DISCUSSION

The plan of action is a key document in the information security program. Organizations develop plans of action that describe how any unimplemented security requirements will be met and how any planned mitigations will be implemented. Organizations can document the system security plan and plan of action as separate or combined documents and in any chosen format.

Federal agencies may consider the submitted system security plans and plans of action as critical inputs to an overall risk management decision to process, store, or transmit CUI on a system hosted by a nonfederal organization and whether it is advisable to pursue an agreement or contract with the nonfederal organization.

<u>3.12.3</u> **Monitor security controls on an ongoing basis to ensure the continued effectiveness of the controls.**

DISCUSSION

Continuous monitoring programs facilitate ongoing awareness of threats, vulnerabilities, and information security to support organizational risk management decisions. The terms continuous and ongoing imply that organizations assess and analyze security controls and information security-related risks at a frequency sufficient to support risk-based decisions. The results of continuous monitoring programs generate appropriate risk response actions by organizations.

Providing access to security information on a continuing basis through reports or dashboards gives organizational officials the capability to make effective and timely risk management decisions.

Automation supports more frequent updates to hardware, software, firmware inventories, and other system information. Effectiveness is further enhanced when continuous monitoring outputs are formatted to provide information that is specific, measurable, actionable, relevant, and timely. Monitoring requirements, including the need for specific monitoring, may also be referenced in other requirements.

[SP 800-137] provides guidance on continuous monitoring.

3.12.4   **Develop, document, and periodically update system security plans that describe system boundaries, system environments of operation, how security requirements are implemented, and the relationships with or connections to other systems.**[28]

DISCUSSION

System security plans relate security requirements to a set of security controls. System security plans also describe, at a high level, how the security controls meet those security requirements, but do not provide detailed, technical descriptions of the design or implementation of the controls. System security plans contain sufficient information to enable a design and implementation that is unambiguously compliant with the intent of the plans and subsequent determinations of risk if the plan is implemented as intended. Security plans need not be single documents; the plans can be a collection of various documents including documents that already exist. Effective security plans make extensive use of references to policies, procedures, and additional documents (e.g., design and implementation specifications) where more detailed information can be obtained. This reduces the documentation requirements associated with security programs and maintains security-related information in other established management/operational areas related to enterprise architecture, system development life cycle, systems engineering, and acquisition.

Federal agencies may consider the submitted system security plans and plans of action as critical inputs to an overall risk management decision to process, store, or transmit CUI on a system hosted by a nonfederal organization and whether it is advisable to pursue an agreement or contract with the nonfederal organization.

[SP 800-18] provides guidance on developing security plans.

Derived Security Requirements

None.

---

[28] There is no prescribed format or specified level of detail for *system security plans*. However, organizations ensure that the required information in 3.12.4 is conveyed in those plans.

3.13 SYSTEM AND COMMUNICATIONS PROTECTION

Basic Security Requirements

3.13.1 **Monitor, control, and protect communications (i.e., information transmitted or received by organizational systems) at the external boundaries and key internal boundaries of organizational systems.**

DISCUSSION

Communications can be monitored, controlled, and protected at boundary components and by restricting or prohibiting interfaces in organizational systems. Boundary components include gateways, routers, firewalls, guards, network-based malicious code analysis and virtualization systems, or encrypted tunnels implemented within a system security architecture (e.g., routers protecting firewalls or application gateways residing on protected subnetworks). Restricting or prohibiting interfaces in organizational systems includes restricting external web communications traffic to designated web servers within managed interfaces and prohibiting external traffic that appears to be spoofing internal addresses.

Organizations consider the shared nature of commercial telecommunications services in the implementation of security requirements associated with the use of such services. Commercial telecommunications services are commonly based on network components and consolidated management systems shared by all attached commercial customers and may also include third party-provided access lines and other service elements. Such transmission services may represent sources of increased risk despite contract security provisions.

[SP 800-41] provides guidance on firewalls and firewall policy. [SP 800-125B] provides guidance on security for virtualization technologies.

3.13.2 **Employ architectural designs, software development techniques, and systems engineering principles that promote effective information security within organizational systems.**

DISCUSSION

Organizations apply systems security engineering principles to new development systems or systems undergoing major upgrades. For legacy systems, organizations apply systems security engineering principles to system upgrades and modifications to the extent feasible, given the current state of hardware, software, and firmware components within those systems. The application of systems security engineering concepts and principles helps to develop trustworthy, secure, and resilient systems and system components and reduce the susceptibility of organizations to disruptions, hazards, and threats. Examples of these concepts and principles include developing layered protections; establishing security policies, architecture, and controls as the foundation for design; incorporating security requirements into the system development life cycle; delineating physical and logical security boundaries; ensuring that developers are trained on how to build secure software; and performing threat modeling to identify use cases, threat agents, attack vectors and patterns, design patterns, and compensating controls needed to mitigate risk. Organizations that apply security engineering concepts and principles can facilitate the development of trustworthy, secure systems, system components, and system services; reduce risk to acceptable levels; and make informed risk-management decisions.

[SP 800-160-1] provides guidance on systems security engineering.

Derived Security Requirements

3.13.3 **Separate user functionality from system management functionality.**

DISCUSSION

System management functionality includes functions necessary to administer databases, network components, workstations, or servers, and typically requires privileged user access. The separation of user functionality from system management functionality is physical or logical. Organizations can implement separation of system management functionality from user functionality by using different computers, different central processing units, different instances of operating systems, or different network addresses; virtualization techniques; or combinations of these or other methods, as appropriate. This type of separation includes web administrative interfaces that use separate authentication methods for users of any other system resources. Separation of system and user functionality may include isolating administrative interfaces on different domains and with additional access controls.

<u>3.13.4</u>   **Prevent unauthorized and unintended information transfer via shared system resources.**

DISCUSSION

The control of information in shared system resources (e.g., registers, cache memory, main memory, hard disks) is also commonly referred to as object reuse and residual information protection. This requirement prevents information produced by the actions of prior users or roles (or the actions of processes acting on behalf of prior users or roles) from being available to any current users or roles (or current processes acting on behalf of current users or roles) that obtain access to shared system resources after those resources have been released back to the system. This requirement also applies to encrypted representations of information. This requirement does not address information remanence, which refers to residual representation of data that has been nominally deleted; covert channels (including storage or timing channels) where shared resources are manipulated to violate information flow restrictions; or components within systems for which there are only single users or roles.

<u>3.13.5</u>   **Implement subnetworks for publicly accessible system components that are physically or logically separated from internal networks.**

DISCUSSION

Subnetworks that are physically or logically separated from internal networks are referred to as demilitarized zones (DMZs). DMZs are typically implemented with boundary control devices and techniques that include routers, gateways, firewalls, virtualization, or cloud-based technologies.

[SP 800-41] provides guidance on firewalls and firewall policy. [SP 800-125B] provides guidance on security for virtualization technologies.

<u>3.13.6</u>   **Deny network communications traffic by default and allow network communications traffic by exception (i.e., deny all, permit by exception).**

DISCUSSION

This requirement applies to inbound and outbound network communications traffic at the system boundary and at identified points within the system. A deny-all, permit-by-exception network communications traffic policy ensures that only those connections which are essential and approved are allowed.

<u>3.13.7</u>   **Prevent remote devices from simultaneously establishing non-remote connections with organizational systems and communicating via some other connection to resources in external networks (i.e., split tunneling).**

DISCUSSION

Split tunneling might be desirable by remote users to communicate with local system resources such as printers or file servers. However, split tunneling allows unauthorized external connections, making the system more vulnerable to attack and to exfiltration of organizational information. This requirement is implemented in remote devices (e.g., notebook computers, smart phones, and tablets) through configuration settings to disable split tunneling in those devices, and by preventing configuration settings from being readily configurable by users. This requirement is implemented in the system by the detection of split tunneling (or of configuration settings that allow split tunneling) in the remote device, and by prohibiting the connection if the remote device is using split tunneling.

3.13.8   **Implement cryptographic mechanisms to prevent unauthorized disclosure of CUI during transmission unless otherwise protected by alternative physical safeguards.**

DISCUSSION

This requirement applies to internal and external networks and any system components that can transmit information including servers, notebook computers, desktop computers, mobile devices, printers, copiers, scanners, and facsimile machines. Communication paths outside the physical protection of controlled boundaries are susceptible to both interception and modification. Organizations relying on commercial providers offering transmission services as commodity services rather than as fully dedicated services (i.e., services which can be highly specialized to individual customer needs), may find it difficult to obtain the necessary assurances regarding the implementation of the controls for transmission confidentiality. In such situations, organizations determine what types of confidentiality services are available in commercial telecommunication service packages. If it is infeasible or impractical to obtain the necessary safeguards and assurances of the effectiveness of the safeguards through appropriate contracting vehicles, organizations implement compensating safeguards or explicitly accept the additional risk. An example of an alternative physical safeguard is a protected distribution system (PDS) where the distribution medium is protected against electronic or physical intercept, thereby ensuring the confidentiality of the information being transmitted. See [NIST CRYPTO].

3.13.9   **Terminate network connections associated with communications sessions at the end of the sessions or after a defined period of inactivity.**

DISCUSSION

This requirement applies to internal and external networks. Terminating network connections associated with communications sessions include de-allocating associated TCP/IP address or port pairs at the operating system level, or de-allocating networking assignments at the application level if multiple application sessions are using a single, operating system-level network connection. Time periods of user inactivity may be established by organizations and include time periods by type of network access or for specific network accesses.

3.13.10   **Establish and manage cryptographic keys for cryptography employed in organizational systems.**

DISCUSSION

Cryptographic key management and establishment can be performed using manual procedures or mechanisms supported by manual procedures. Organizations define key management requirements in accordance with applicable federal laws, Executive Orders, policies, directives, regulations, and standards specifying appropriate options, levels, and parameters.

[SP 800-56A] and [SP 800-57-1] provide guidance on cryptographic key management and key establishment.

3.13.11   **Employ FIPS-validated cryptography when used to protect the confidentiality of CUI.**

DISCUSSION

Cryptography can be employed to support many security solutions including the protection of controlled unclassified information, the provision of digital signatures, and the enforcement of information separation when authorized individuals have the necessary clearances for such information but lack the necessary formal access approvals. Cryptography can also be used to support random number generation and hash generation. Generally applicable cryptographic standards include FIPS-validated cryptography and/or NSA-approved cryptography. See [NIST CRYPTO]; [NIST CAVP]; and [NIST CMVP].

3.13.12   **Prohibit remote activation of collaborative computing devices and provide indication of devices in use to users present at the device.**[29]

DISCUSSION

Collaborative computing devices include networked white boards, cameras, and microphones. Indication of use includes signals to users when collaborative computing devices are activated. Dedicated video conferencing systems, which rely on one of the participants calling or connecting to the other party to activate the video conference, are excluded.

3.13.13   **Control and monitor the use of mobile code.**

DISCUSSION

Mobile code technologies include Java, JavaScript, ActiveX, Postscript, PDF, Shockwave movies, Flash animations, and VBScript. Decisions regarding the use of mobile code in organizational systems are based on the potential for the code to cause damage to the systems if used maliciously. Usage restrictions and implementation guidance apply to the selection and use of mobile code installed on servers and mobile code downloaded and executed on individual workstations, notebook computers, and devices (e.g., smart phones). Mobile code policy and procedures address controlling or preventing the development, acquisition, or introduction of unacceptable mobile code in systems, including requiring mobile code to be digitally signed by a trusted source.

[SP 800-28] provides guidance on mobile code.

3.13.14   **Control and monitor the use of Voice over Internet Protocol (VoIP) technologies.**

DISCUSSION

VoIP has different requirements, features, functionality, availability, and service limitations when compared with the Plain Old Telephone Service (POTS) (i.e., the standard telephone service). In contrast, other telephone services are based on high-speed, digital communications lines, such as Integrated Services Digital Network (ISDN) and Fiber Distributed Data Interface (FDDI). The main distinctions between POTS and non-POTS services are speed and bandwidth. To address the threats associated with VoIP, usage restrictions and implementation guidelines are based on the potential for the VoIP technology to cause damage to the system if it is used maliciously. Threats to VoIP are similar to those inherent with any Internet-based application.

[SP 800-58] provides guidance on Voice Over IP Systems.

---

[29] Dedicated video conferencing systems, which rely on one of the participants calling or connecting to the other party to activate the video conference, are excluded.

3.13.15 **Protect the authenticity of communications sessions.**

DISCUSSION

Authenticity protection includes protecting against man-in-the-middle attacks, session hijacking, and the insertion of false information into communications sessions. This requirement addresses communications protection at the session versus packet level (e.g., sessions in service-oriented architectures providing web-based services) and establishes grounds for confidence at both ends of communications sessions in ongoing identities of other parties and in the validity of information transmitted.

[SP 800-77], [SP 800-95], and [SP 800-113] provide guidance on secure communications sessions.

3.13.16 **Protect the confidentiality of CUI at rest.**

DISCUSSION

Information at rest refers to the state of information when it is not in process or in transit and is located on storage devices as specific components of systems. The focus of protection at rest is not on the type of storage device or the frequency of access but rather the state of the information. Organizations can use different mechanisms to achieve confidentiality protections, including the use of cryptographic mechanisms and file share scanning. Organizations may also use other controls including secure off-line storage in lieu of online storage when adequate protection of information at rest cannot otherwise be achieved or continuous monitoring to identify malicious code at rest. See [NIST CRYPTO].

3.14 SYSTEM AND INFORMATION INTEGRITY

Basic Security Requirements

3.14.1 **Identify, report, and correct system flaws in a timely manner.**

DISCUSSION

Organizations identify systems that are affected by announced software and firmware flaws including potential vulnerabilities resulting from those flaws and report this information to designated personnel with information security responsibilities. Security-relevant updates include patches, service packs, hot fixes, and anti-virus signatures. Organizations address flaws discovered during security assessments, continuous monitoring, incident response activities, and system error handling. Organizations can take advantage of available resources such as the Common Weakness Enumeration (CWE) database or Common Vulnerabilities and Exposures (CVE) database in remediating flaws discovered in organizational systems.

Organization-defined time periods for updating security-relevant software and firmware may vary based on a variety of factors including the criticality of the update (i.e., severity of the vulnerability related to the discovered flaw). Some types of flaw remediation may require more testing than other types of remediation.

[SP 800-40] provides guidance on patch management technologies.

3.14.2 **Provide protection from malicious code at designated locations within organizational systems.**

DISCUSSION

Designated locations include system entry and exit points which may include firewalls, remote-access servers, workstations, electronic mail servers, web servers, proxy servers, notebook computers, and mobile devices. Malicious code includes viruses, worms, Trojan horses, and spyware. Malicious code can be encoded in various formats (e.g., UUENCODE, Unicode), contained within compressed or hidden files, or hidden in files using techniques such as steganography. Malicious code can be inserted into systems in a variety of ways including web accesses, electronic mail, electronic mail attachments, and portable storage devices. Malicious code insertions occur through the exploitation of system vulnerabilities.

Malicious code protection mechanisms include anti-virus signature definitions and reputation-based technologies. A variety of technologies and methods exist to limit or eliminate the effects of malicious code. Pervasive configuration management and comprehensive software integrity controls may be effective in preventing execution of unauthorized code. In addition to commercial off-the-shelf software, malicious code may also be present in custom-built software. This could include logic bombs, back doors, and other types of cyber-attacks that could affect organizational missions/business functions. Traditional malicious code protection mechanisms cannot always detect such code. In these situations, organizations rely instead on other safeguards including secure coding practices, configuration management and control, trusted procurement processes, and monitoring practices to help ensure that software does not perform functions other than the functions intended.

[SP 800-83] provides guidance on malware incident prevention.

3.14.3 **Monitor system security alerts and advisories and take action in response.**

DISCUSSION

There are many publicly available sources of system security alerts and advisories. The United States Computer Emergency Readiness Team (US-CERT) generates security alerts and advisories to maintain situational awareness across the federal government and in nonfederal organizations.

Software vendors, subscription services, and relevant industry information sharing and analysis centers (ISACs) may also provide security alerts and advisories. Examples of response actions include notifying relevant external organizations, for example, external mission/business partners, supply chain partners, external service providers, and peer or supporting organizations

[SP 800-161] provides guidance on supply chain risk management.

Derived Security Requirements

3.14.4   **Update malicious code protection mechanisms when new releases are available.**

DISCUSSION

Malicious code protection mechanisms include anti-virus signature definitions and reputation-based technologies. A variety of technologies and methods exist to limit or eliminate the effects of malicious code. Pervasive configuration management and comprehensive software integrity controls may be effective in preventing execution of unauthorized code. In addition to commercial off-the-shelf software, malicious code may also be present in custom-built software. This could include logic bombs, back doors, and other types of cyber-attacks that could affect organizational missions/business functions. Traditional malicious code protection mechanisms cannot always detect such code. In these situations, organizations rely instead on other safeguards including secure coding practices, configuration management and control, trusted procurement processes, and monitoring practices to help ensure that software does not perform functions other than the functions intended.

3.14.5   **Perform periodic scans of organizational systems and real-time scans of files from external sources as files are downloaded, opened, or executed.**

DISCUSSION

Periodic scans of organizational systems and real-time scans of files from external sources can detect malicious code. Malicious code can be encoded in various formats (e.g., UUENCODE, Unicode), contained within compressed or hidden files, or hidden in files using techniques such as steganography. Malicious code can be inserted into systems in a variety of ways including web accesses, electronic mail, electronic mail attachments, and portable storage devices. Malicious code insertions occur through the exploitation of system vulnerabilities.

Malicious code protection mechanisms include anti-virus signature definitions and reputation-based technologies. Many technologies and methods exist to limit or eliminate the effects of malicious code. Pervasive configuration management and comprehensive software integrity controls may be effective in preventing execution of unauthorized code. In addition to commercial off-the-shelf software, malicious code may also be present in custom-built software. This could include logic bombs, back doors, and other types of cyber-attacks that could affect organizational missions/business functions. Traditional malicious code protection mechanisms cannot always detect such code. In these situations, organizations rely instead on other safeguards including secure coding practices, configuration management and control, trusted procurement processes, and monitoring practices to help ensure that software does not perform functions other than the functions intended.

3.14.6   **Monitor organizational systems, including inbound and outbound communications traffic, to detect attacks and indicators of potential attacks.**

DISCUSSION

System monitoring includes external and internal monitoring. External monitoring includes the observation of events occurring at the system boundary (i.e., part of perimeter defense and boundary protection). Internal monitoring includes the observation of events occurring within the system. Organizations can monitor systems, for example, by observing audit record activities in real time or by observing other system aspects such as access patterns, characteristics of access, and other actions. The monitoring objectives may guide determination of the events. System monitoring capability is achieved through a variety of tools and techniques (e.g., intrusion detection systems, intrusion prevention systems, malicious code protection software, scanning tools, audit record monitoring software, network monitoring software). Strategic locations for monitoring devices include selected perimeter locations and near server farms supporting critical applications, with such devices being employed at managed system interfaces. The granularity of monitoring information collected is based on organizational monitoring objectives and the capability of systems to support such objectives.

System monitoring is an integral part of continuous monitoring and incident response programs. Output from system monitoring serves as input to continuous monitoring and incident response programs. A network connection is any connection with a device that communicates through a network (e.g., local area network, Internet). A remote connection is any connection with a device communicating through an external network (e.g., the Internet). Local, network, and remote connections can be either wired or wireless.

Unusual or unauthorized activities or conditions related to inbound/outbound communications traffic include internal traffic that indicates the presence of malicious code in systems or propagating among system components, the unauthorized exporting of information, or signaling to external systems. Evidence of malicious code is used to identify potentially compromised systems or system components. System monitoring requirements, including the need for specific types of system monitoring, may be referenced in other requirements.

[SP 800-94] provides guidance on intrusion detection and prevention systems.

3.14.7 Identify unauthorized use of organizational systems.

DISCUSSION

System monitoring includes external and internal monitoring. System monitoring can detect unauthorized use of organizational systems. System monitoring is an integral part of continuous monitoring and incident response programs. Monitoring is achieved through a variety of tools and techniques (e.g., intrusion detection systems, intrusion prevention systems, malicious code protection software, scanning tools, audit record monitoring software, network monitoring software). Output from system monitoring serves as input to continuous monitoring and incident response programs.

Unusual/unauthorized activities or conditions related to inbound and outbound communications traffic include internal traffic that indicates the presence of malicious code in systems or propagating among system components, the unauthorized exporting of information, or signaling to external systems. Evidence of malicious code is used to identify potentially compromised systems or system components. System monitoring requirements, including the need for specific types of system monitoring, may be referenced in other requirements.

[SP 800-94] provides guidance on intrusion detection and prevention systems.

APPENDIX A

REFERENCES

LAWS, EXECUTIVE ORDERS, REGULATIONS, INSTRUCTIONS, STANDARDS, AND GUIDELINES[30]

LAWS AND EXECUTIVE ORDERS

[ATOM54]	Atomic Energy Act (P.L. 83-703), August 1954. https://www.govinfo.gov/app/details/STATUTE-68/STATUTE-68-Pg919
[FOIA96]	Freedom of Information Act (FOIA), 5 U.S.C. § 552, As Amended By Public Law No. 104-231, 110 Stat. 3048, Electronic Freedom of Information Act Amendments of 1996. https://www.govinfo.gov/app/details/PLAW-104publ231
[FISMA]	Federal Information Security Modernization Act (P.L. 113-283), December 2014. https://www.govinfo.gov/app/details/PLAW-113publ283
[40 USC 11331]	Title 40 U.S. Code, Sec. 11331, Responsibilities for Federal information systems standards. 2017 ed. https://www.govinfo.gov/app/details/USCODE-2017-title40/USCODE-2017-title40-subtitleIII-chap113-subchapIII-sec11331
[44 USC 3502]	Title 44 U.S. Code, Sec. 3502, Definitions. 2017 ed. https://www.govinfo.gov/app/details/USCODE-2017-title44/USCODE-2017-title44-chap35-subchapI-sec3502
[44 USC 3552]	Title 44 U.S. Code, Sec. 3552, Definitions. 2017 ed. https://www.govinfo.gov/app/details/USCODE-2017-title44/USCODE-2017-title44-chap35-subchapII-sec3552
[44 USC 3554]	Title 44 U.S. Code, Sec. 3554, Federal agency responsibilities. 2017 ed. https://www.govinfo.gov/app/details/USCODE-2017-title44/USCODE-2017-title44-chap35-subchapII-sec3554
[EO 13526]	Executive Order 13526 (2009) Classified National Security Information. (The White House, Washington, DC), DCPD-200901022, December 29, 2009. https://www.govinfo.gov/app/details/DCPD-200901022
[EO 13556]	Executive Order 13556 (2010) Controlled Unclassified Information. (The White House, Washington, DC), DCPD-201000942, November 4, 2010. https://www.govinfo.gov/app/details/DCPD-201000942

POLICIES, REGULATIONS, DIRECTIVES, AND INSTRUCTIONS

[32 CFR 2002]	32 CFR Part 2002, Controlled Unclassified Information, September 2016. https://www.govinfo.gov/app/details/CFR-2017-title32-vol6/CFR-2017-title32-vol6-part2002/summary

---

[30] References in this section without specific publication dates or revision numbers are assumed to refer to the most recent updates to those publications.

[OMB A-130]   Office of Management and Budget (2016) Managing Information as a
               Strategic Resource. (The White House, Washington, DC), OMB Circular A-
               130, July 2016.
               https://www.whitehouse.gov/sites/whitehouse.gov/files/omb/circulars/A130/a13
               0revised.pdf

[CNSSI 4009]   Committee on National Security Systems (2015) Committee on National
               Security Systems (CNSS) Glossary. (National Security Agency, Fort George G.
               Meade, MD), CNSS Instruction 4009.
               https://www.cnss.gov/CNSS/issuances/Instructions.cfm

STANDARDS, GUIDELINES, AND REPORTS

[ISO 27001]   International Organization for Standardization/International
               Electrotechnical Commission (2013) Information Technology—Security
               techniques— Information security management systems—Requirements.
               (International Organization for Standardization, Geneva, Switzerland),
               ISO/IEC 27001:2013.
               https://www.iso.org/standard/54534.html

[FIPS 140-2]   National Institute of Standards and Technology (2001) Security
               Requirements for Cryptographic Modules. (U.S. Department of Commerce,
               Washington, DC), Federal Information Processing Standards Publication
               (FIPS) 140-2, Change Notice 2 December 3, 2002.
               https://doi.org/10.6028/NIST.FIPS.140-2

[FIPS 140-3]   National Institute of Standards and Technology (2019) Security
               Requirements for Cryptographic Modules. (U.S. Department of Commerce,
               Washington, DC), Federal Information Processing Standards Publication
               (FIPS) 140-3.
               https://doi.org/10.6028/NIST.FIPS.140-3

[FIPS 199]   National Institute of Standards and Technology (2004) Standards for
               Security Categorization of Federal Information and Information Systems.
               (U.S. Department of Commerce, Washington, DC), Federal Information
               Processing Standards Publication (FIPS) 199.
               https://doi.org/10.6028/NIST.FIPS.199

[FIPS 200]   National Institute of Standards and Technology (2006) Minimum Security
               Requirements for Federal Information and Information Systems. (U.S.
               Department of Commerce, Washington, DC), Federal Information
               Processing Standards Publication (FIPS) 200.
               https://doi.org/10.6028/NIST.FIPS.200

[SP 800-18]   Swanson MA, Hash J, Bowen P (2006) Guide for Developing Security Plans
               for Federal Information Systems. (National Institute of Standards and
               Technology, Gaithersburg, MD), NIST Special Publication (SP) 800-18, Rev.
               1.
               https://doi.org/10.6028/NIST.SP.800-18r1

[SP 800-28]   Jansen W, Winograd T, Scarfone KA (2008) Guidelines on Active Content and Mobile Code. (National Institute of Standards and Technology, Gaithersburg, MD), NIST Special Publication (SP) 800-28, Version 2. https://doi.org/10.6028/NIST.SP.800-28ver2

[SP 800-30]   Joint Task Force Transformation Initiative (2012) Guide for Conducting Risk Assessments. (National Institute of Standards and Technology, Gaithersburg, MD), NIST Special Publication (SP) 800-30, Rev. 1. https://doi.org/10.6028/NIST.SP.800-30r1

[SP 800-39]   Joint Task Force Transformation Initiative (2011) Managing Information Security Risk: Organization, Mission, and Information System View. (National Institute of Standards and Technology, Gaithersburg, MD), NIST Special Publication (SP) 800-39. https://doi.org/10.6028/NIST.SP.800-39

[SP 800-40]   Souppaya MP, Scarfone KA (2013) Guide to Enterprise Patch Management Technologies. (National Institute of Standards and Technology, Gaithersburg, MD), NIST Special Publication (SP) 800-40, Rev. 3. https://doi.org/10.6028/NIST.SP.800-40r3

[SP 800-41]   Scarfone KA, Hoffman P (2009) Guidelines on Firewalls and Firewall Policy. (National Institute of Standards and Technology, Gaithersburg, MD), NIST Special Publication (SP) 800-41, Rev. 1. https://doi.org/10.6028/NIST.SP.800-41r1

[SP 800-46]   Souppaya MP, Scarfone KA (2016) Guide to Enterprise Telework, Remote Access, and Bring Your Own Device (BYOD) Security. (National Institute of Standards and Technology, Gaithersburg, MD), NIST Special Publication (SP) 800-46, Rev. 2. https://doi.org/10.6028/NIST.SP.800-46r2

[SP 800-50]   Wilson M, Hash J (2003) Building an Information Technology Security Awareness and Training Program. (National Institute of Standards and Technology, Gaithersburg, MD), NIST Special Publication (SP) 800-50. https://doi.org/10.6028/NIST.SP.800-50

[SP 800-53]   Joint Task Force Transformation Initiative (2013) Security and Privacy Controls for Federal Information Systems and Organizations. (National Institute of Standards and Technology, Gaithersburg, MD), NIST Special Publication (SP) 800-53, Rev. 4, Includes updates as of January 22, 2015. https://doi.org/10.6028/NIST.SP.800-53r4

[SP 800-53A]   Joint Task Force Transformation Initiative (2014) Assessing Security and Privacy Controls in Federal Information Systems and Organizations: Building Effective Assessment Plans. (National Institute of Standards and Technology, Gaithersburg, MD), NIST Special Publication (SP) 800-53A, Rev. 4, Includes updates as of December 18, 2014. https://doi.org/10.6028/NIST.SP.800-53Ar4

[SP 800-53B]   Control Baselines and Tailoring Guidance for Federal Information Systems
                 and Organizations. (National Institute of Standards and Technology,
                 Gaithersburg, MD), Draft NIST Special Publication (SP) 800-53B.
                 [Forthcoming].

[SP 800-56A]   Barker EB, Chen L, Roginsky A, Vassilev A, Davis R (2018) Recommendation
                 for Pair-Wise Key-Establishment Schemes Using Discrete Logarithm
                 Cryptography. (National Institute of Standards and Technology,
                 Gaithersburg, MD), NIST Special Publication (SP) 800-56A, Rev. 3.
                 https://doi.org/10.6028/NIST.SP.800-56Ar3

[SP 800-57-1]   Barker EB (2016) Recommendation for Key Management, Part 1: General.
                 (National Institute of Standards and Technology, Gaithersburg, MD), NIST
                 Special Publication (SP) 800-57 Part 1, Rev. 4.
                 https://doi.org/10.6028/NIST.SP.800-57pt1r4

[SP 800-58]   Kuhn R, Walsh TJ, Fries S (2005) Security Considerations for Voice Over IP
                 Systems. (National Institute of Standards and Technology, Gaithersburg,
                 MD), NIST Special Publication (SP) 800-58.
                 https://doi.org/10.6028/NIST.SP.800-58

[SP 800-60-1]   Stine KM, Kissel RL, Barker WC, Fahlsing J, Gulick J (2008) Guide for
                 Mapping Types of Information and Information Systems to Security
                 Categories. (National Institute of Standards and Technology, Gaithersburg,
                 MD), NIST Special Publication (SP) 800-60, Vol. 1, Rev. 1.
                 https://doi.org/10.6028/NIST.SP.800-60v1r1

[SP 800-60-2]   Stine KM, Kissel RL, Barker WC, Lee A, Fahlsing J (2008) Guide for Mapping
                 Types of Information and Information Systems to Security Categories:
                 Appendices. (National Institute of Standards and Technology, Gaithersburg,
                 MD), NIST Special Publication (SP) 800-60, Vol. 2, Rev. 1.
                 https://doi.org/10.6028/NIST.SP.800-60v2r1

[SP 800-61]   Cichonski PR, Millar T, Grance T, Scarfone KA (2012) Computer Security
                 Incident Handling Guide. (National Institute of Standards and Technology,
                 Gaithersburg, MD), NIST Special Publication (SP) 800-61, Rev. 2.
                 https://doi.org/10.6028/NIST.SP.800-61r2

[SP 800-63-3]   Grassi PA, Garcia ME, Fenton JL (2017) Digital Identity Guidelines. (National
                 Institute of Standards and Technology, Gaithersburg, MD), NIST Special
                 Publication (SP) 800-63-3, Includes updates as of December 1, 2017.
                 https://doi.org/10.6028/NIST.SP.800-63-3

[SP 800-70]   Quinn SD, Souppaya MP, Cook MR, Scarfone KA (2018) National Checklist
                 Program for IT Products: Guidelines for Checklist Users and Developers.
                 (National Institute of Standards and Technology, Gaithersburg, MD), NIST
                 Special Publication (SP) 800-70, Rev. 4.
                 https://doi.org/10.6028/NIST.SP.800-70r4

[SP 800-77]   Frankel SE, Kent K, Lewkowski R, Orebaugh AD, Ritchey RW, Sharma SR
                 (2005) Guide to IPsec VPNs. (National Institute of Standards and
                 Technology, Gaithersburg, MD), NIST Special Publication (SP) 800-77.
                 https://doi.org/10.6028/NIST.SP.800-77

[SP 800-83]   Souppaya MP, Scarfone KA (2013) Guide to Malware Incident Prevention
                   and Handling for Desktops and Laptops. (National Institute of Standards
                   and Technology, Gaithersburg, MD), NIST Special Publication (SP) 800-83,
                   Rev. 1.
                   https://doi.org/10.6028/NIST.SP.800-83r1

[SP 800-84]   Grance T, Nolan T, Burke K, Dudley R, White G, Good T (2006) Guide to Test,
                   Training, and Exercise Programs for IT Plans and Capabilities. (National
                   Institute of Standards and Technology, Gaithersburg, MD), NIST Special
                   Publication (SP) 800-84.
                   https://doi.org/10.6028/NIST.SP.800-84

[SP 800-86]   Kent K, Chevalier S, Grance T, Dang H (2006) Guide to Integrating Forensic
                   Techniques into Incident Response. (National Institute of Standards and
                   Technology, Gaithersburg, MD), NIST Special Publication (SP) 800-86.
                   https://doi.org/10.6028/NIST.SP.800-86

[SP 800-88]   Kissel RL, Regenscheid AR, Scholl MA, Stine KM (2014) Guidelines for Media
                   Sanitization. (National Institute of Standards and Technology, Gaithersburg,
                   MD), NIST Special Publication (SP) 800-88, Rev. 1.
                   https://doi.org/10.6028/NIST.SP.800-88r1

[SP 800-92]   Kent K, Souppaya MP (2006) Guide to Computer Security Log Management.
                   (National Institute of Standards and Technology, Gaithersburg, MD), NIST
                   Special Publication (SP) 800-92.
                   https://doi.org/10.6028/NIST.SP.800-92

[SP 800-94]   Scarfone KA, Mell PM (2007) Guide to Intrusion Detection and Prevention
                   Systems (IDPS). (National Institute of Standards and Technology,
                   Gaithersburg, MD), NIST Special Publication (SP) 800-94.
                   https://doi.org/10.6028/NIST.SP.800-94

[SP 800-95]   Singhal A, Winograd T, Scarfone KA (2007) Guide to Secure Web Services.
                   (National Institute of Standards and Technology, Gaithersburg, MD), NIST
                   Special Publication (SP) 800-95.
                   https://doi.org/10.6028/NIST.SP.800-95

[SP 800-97]   Frankel SE, Eydt B, Owens L, Scarfone KA (2007) Establishing Wireless
                   Robust Security Networks: A Guide to IEEE 802.11i. (National Institute of
                   Standards and Technology, Gaithersburg, MD), NIST Special Publication (SP)
                   800-97.
                   https://doi.org/10.6028/NIST.SP.800-97

[SP 800-101]   Ayers RP, Brothers S, Jansen W (2014) Guidelines on Mobile Device
                   Forensics. (National Institute of Standards and Technology, Gaithersburg,
                   MD), NIST Special Publication (SP) 800-101, Rev. 1.
                   https://doi.org/10.6028/NIST.SP.800-101r1

[SP 800-111]   Scarfone KA, Souppaya MP, Sexton M (2007) Guide to Storage Encryption
                   Technologies for End User Devices. (National Institute of Standards and
                   Technology, Gaithersburg, MD), NIST Special Publication (SP) 800-111.
                   https://doi.org/10.6028/NIST.SP.800-111

[SP 800-113]   Frankel SE, Hoffman P, Orebaugh AD, Park R (2008) Guide to SSL VPNs.
                  (National Institute of Standards and Technology, Gaithersburg, MD), NIST
                  Special Publication (SP) 800-113.
                  https://doi.org/10.6028/NIST.SP.800-113

[SP 800-114]   Souppaya MP, Scarfone KA (2016) User's Guide to Telework and Bring Your
                  Own Device (BYOD) Security. (National Institute of Standards and
                  Technology, Gaithersburg, MD), NIST Special Publication (SP) 800-114, Rev.
                  1.
                  https://doi.org/10.6028/NIST.SP.800-114r1

[SP 800-124]   Souppaya MP, Scarfone KA (2013) Guidelines for Managing the Security of
                  Mobile Devices in the Enterprise. (National Institute of Standards and
                  Technology, Gaithersburg, MD), NIST Special Publication (SP) 800-124, Rev.
                  1.
                  https://doi.org/10.6028/NIST.SP.800-124r1

[SP 800-125B]   Chandramouli R (2016) Secure Virtual Network Configuration for Virtual
                  Machine (VM) Protection. (National Institute of Standards and Technology,
                  Gaithersburg, MD), NIST Special Publication (SP) 800-125B.
                  https://doi.org/10.6028/NIST.SP.800-125B

[SP 800-128]   Johnson LA, Dempsey KL, Ross RS, Gupta S, Bailey D (2011) Guide for
                  Security-Focused Configuration Management of Information Systems.
                  (National Institute of Standards and Technology, Gaithersburg, MD), NIST
                  Special Publication (SP) 800-128.
                  https://doi.org/10.6028/NIST.SP.800-128

[SP 800-137]   Dempsey KL, Chawla NS, Johnson LA, Johnston R, Jones AC, Orebaugh AD,
                  Scholl MA, Stine KM (2011) Information Security Continuous Monitoring
                  (ISCM) for Federal Information Systems and Organizations. (National
                  Institute of Standards and Technology, Gaithersburg, MD), NIST Special
                  Publication (SP) 800-137.
                  https://doi.org/10.6028/NIST.SP.800-137

[SP 800-160-1]   Ross RS, Oren JC, McEvilley M (2016) Systems Security Engineering:
                  Considerations for a Multidisciplinary Approach in the Engineering of
                  Trustworthy Secure Systems. (National Institute of Standards and
                  Technology, Gaithersburg, MD), NIST Special Publication (SP) 800-160, Vol.
                  1, Includes updates as of March 21, 2018.
                  https://doi.org/10.6028/NIST.SP.800-160v1

[SP 800-161]   Boyens JM, Paulsen C, Moorthy R, Bartol N (2015) Supply Chain Risk
                  Management Practices for Federal Information Systems and Organizations.
                  (National Institute of Standards and Technology, Gaithersburg, MD), NIST
                  Special Publication (SP) 800-161.
                  https://doi.org/10.6028/NIST.SP.800-161

[SP 800-167]   Sedgewick A, Souppaya MP, Scarfone KA (2015) Guide to Application
                  Whitelisting. (National Institute of Standards and Technology, Gaithersburg,
                  MD), NIST Special Publication (SP) 800-167.
                  https://doi.org/10.6028/NIST.SP.800-167

[SP 800-171A]   Ross RS, Dempsey KL, Pillitteri VY (2018) Assessing Security Requirements for Controlled Unclassified Information. (National Institute of Standards and Technology, Gaithersburg, MD), NIST Special Publication (SP) 800-171A.
https://doi.org/10.6028/NIST.SP.800-171A

[SP 800-181]   Newhouse WD, Witte GA, Scribner B, Keith S (2017) National Initiative for Cybersecurity Education (NICE) Cybersecurity Workforce Framework. (National Institute of Standards and Technology, Gaithersburg, MD), NIST Special Publication (SP) 800-181.
https://doi.org/10.6028/NIST.SP.800-181

MISCELLANEOUS PUBLICATIONS AND WEBSITES

[GAO 19-128]   U.S. Government Accountability Office (2018) Weapons Systems Cybersecurity. Report to the Committee on Armed Services, U.S. Senate (Washington, DC), GAO 19-128.
https://www.gao.gov/assets/700/694913.pdf

[IETF 5905]   Mills D, Martin J (ed.), Burbank J, Kasch W (2010) Network Time Protocol Version 4: Protocol and Algorithms Specification. (Internet Engineering Task Force), IETF Request for Comments (RFC) 5905.
https://doi.org/10.17487/RFC5905

[NARA CUI]   National Archives and Records Administration (2019) *Controlled Unclassified Information (CUI) Registry.*
https://www.archives.gov/cui

[NARA MARK]   National Archives and Records Administration (2016) Marking Controlled Unclassified Information, Version 1.1. (National Archives, Washington, DC).
https://www.archives.gov/files/cui/20161206-cui-marking-handbook-v1-1.pdf

[NIST CAVP]   National Institute of Standards and Technology (2019) *Cryptographic Algorithm Validation Program.*
https://csrc.nist.gov/projects/cavp

[NIST CMVP]   National Institute of Standards and Technology (2019) *Cryptographic Module Validation Program.*
https://csrc.nist.gov/projects/cmvp

[NIST CRYPTO]   National Institute of Standards and Technology (2019) *Cryptographic Standards and Guidelines.*
https://csrc.nist.gov/projects/cryptographic-standards-and-guidelines

[NIST CSF]   National Institute of Standards and Technology (2018) Framework for Improving Critical Infrastructure Cybersecurity, Version 1.1. (National Institute of Standards and Technology, Gaithersburg, MD).
https://doi.org/10.6028/NIST.CSWP.04162018

[NIST CUI]   National Institute of Standards and Technology (2019) *Special Publication 800-171 Publication and Supporting Resources.*
https://csrc.nist.gov/publications/detail/sp/800-171/rev-1/final

GLOSSARY

COMMON TERMS AND DEFINITIONS

Appendix B provides definitions for security terminology used within Special Publication 800-171. Unless specifically defined in this glossary, all terms used in this publication are consistent with the definitions contained in [CNSSI 4009] *National Information Assurance Glossary*.

agency [OMB A-130]	Any executive agency or department, military department, Federal Government corporation, Federal Government-controlled corporation, or other establishment in the Executive Branch of the Federal Government, or any independent regulatory agency.
assessment	See *security control assessment*.
assessor	See *security control assessor*.
audit log	A chronological record of system activities, including records of system accesses and operations performed in a given period.
audit record	An individual entry in an audit log related to an audited event.
authentication [FIPS 200, Adapted]	Verifying the identity of a user, process, or device, often as a prerequisite to allowing access to resources in a system.
availability [44 USC 3552]	Ensuring timely and reliable access to and use of information.
advanced persistent threat [SP 800-39]	An adversary that possesses sophisticated levels of expertise and significant resources which allow it to create opportunities to achieve its objectives by using multiple attack vectors including, for example, cyber, physical, and deception. These objectives typically include establishing and extending footholds within the IT infrastructure of the targeted organizations for purposes of exfiltrating information, undermining or impeding critical aspects of a mission, program, or organization; or positioning itself to carry out these objectives in the future. The advanced persistent threat pursues its objectives repeatedly over an extended period; adapts to defenders' efforts to resist it; and is determined to maintain the level of interaction needed to execute its objectives.
baseline configuration	A documented set of specifications for a system, or a configuration item within a system, that has been formally reviewed and agreed on at a given point in time, and which can be changed only through change control procedures.

bidirectional authentication	Two parties authenticating each other at the same time. Also known as mutual authentication or two-way authentication.
blacklisting	A process used to identify software programs that are not authorized to execute on a system or prohibited Universal Resource Locators (URL)/websites.
confidentiality [44 USC 3552]	Preserving authorized restrictions on information access and disclosure, including means for protecting personal privacy and proprietary information.
configuration management	A collection of activities focused on establishing and maintaining the integrity of information technology products and systems, through control of processes for initializing, changing, and monitoring the configurations of those products and systems throughout the system development life cycle.
configuration settings	The set of parameters that can be changed in hardware, software, or firmware that affect the security posture and/or functionality of the system.
controlled area	Any area or space for which the organization has confidence that the physical and procedural protections provided are sufficient to meet the requirements established for protecting the information or system.
controlled unclassified information [EO 13556]	Information that law, regulation, or governmentwide policy requires to have safeguarding or disseminating controls, excluding information that is classified under Executive Order 13526, *Classified National Security Information*, December 29, 2009, or any predecessor or successor order, or the Atomic Energy Act of 1954, as amended.
CUI categories [32 CFR 2002]	Those types of information for which laws, regulations, or governmentwide policies require or permit agencies to exercise safeguarding or dissemination controls, and which the CUI Executive Agent has approved and listed in the CUI Registry.
CUI Executive Agent [32 CFR 2002]	The National Archives and Records Administration (NARA), which implements the executive branch-wide CUI Program and oversees federal agency actions to comply with Executive Order 13556. NARA has delegated this authority to the Director of the Information Security Oversight Office (ISOO).
CUI program [32 CFR 2002]	The executive branch-wide program to standardize CUI handling by all federal agencies. The program includes the rules, organization, and procedures for CUI, established by Executive Order 13556, 32 CFR Part 2002, and the CUI Registry.

CUI registry
[32 CFR 2002]

The online repository for all information, guidance, policy, and requirements on handling CUI, including everything issued by the CUI Executive Agent other than 32 CFR Part 2002. Among other information, the CUI Registry identifies all approved CUI categories, provides general descriptions for each, identifies the basis for controls, establishes markings, and includes guidance on handling procedures.

cyber-physical systems

Interacting digital, analog, physical, and human components engineered for function through integrated physics and logic.

dual authorization
[CNSSI 4009, Adapted]

The system of storage and handling designed to prohibit individual access to certain resources by requiring the presence and actions of at least two authorized persons, each capable of detecting incorrect or unauthorized security procedures with respect to the task being performed.

executive agency
[OMB A-130]

An executive department specified in 5 U.S.C. Sec. 101; a military department specified in 5 U.S.C. Sec. 102; an independent establishment as defined in 5 U.S.C. Sec. 104(1); and a wholly owned Government corporation fully subject to the provisions of 31 U.S.C. Chapter 91.

external system (or component)

A system or component of a system that is outside of the authorization boundary established by the organization and for which the organization typically has no direct control over the application of required security controls or the assessment of security control effectiveness.

external system service

A system service that is implemented outside of the authorization boundary of the organizational system (i.e., a service that is used by, but not a part of, the organizational system) and for which the organization typically has no direct control over the application of required security controls or the assessment of security control effectiveness.

external system service provider

A provider of external system services to an organization through a variety of consumer-producer relationships including but not limited to: joint ventures; business partnerships; outsourcing arrangements (i.e., through contracts, interagency agreements, lines of business arrangements); licensing agreements; and/or supply chain exchanges.

external network

A network not controlled by the organization.

federal agency

See *executive agency*.

federal information system
[40 USC 11331]

An information system used or operated by an executive agency, by a contractor of an executive agency, or by another organization on behalf of an executive agency.

FIPS-validated cryptography	A cryptographic module validated by the Cryptographic Module Validation Program (CMVP) to meet requirements specified in FIPS Publication 140-2 (as amended). As a prerequisite to CMVP validation, the cryptographic module is required to employ a cryptographic algorithm implementation that has successfully passed validation testing by the Cryptographic Algorithm Validation Program (CAVP). See *NSA-approved cryptography*.
firmware [CNSSI 4009]	Computer programs and data stored in hardware - typically in read-only memory (ROM) or programmable read-only memory (PROM) - such that the programs and data cannot be dynamically written or modified during execution of the programs. See *hardware* and *software*.
hardware [CNSSI 4009]	The material physical components of a system. See *software* and *firmware*.
identifier	Unique data used to represent a person's identity and associated attributes. A name or a card number are examples of identifiers. A unique label used by a system to indicate a specific entity, object, or group.
impact	With respect to security, the effect on organizational operations, organizational assets, individuals, other organizations, or the Nation (including the national security interests of the United States) of a loss of confidentiality, integrity, or availability of information or a system. With respect to privacy, the adverse effects that individuals could experience when an information system processes their PII.
impact value [FIPS 199]	The assessed worst-case potential impact that could result from a compromise of the confidentiality, integrity, or availability of information expressed as a value of low, moderate or high.
incident [44 USC 3552]	An occurrence that actually or imminently jeopardizes, without lawful authority, the confidentiality, integrity, or availability of information or an information system; or constitutes a violation or imminent threat of violation of law, security policies, security procedures, or acceptable use policies.
information [OMB A-130]	Any communication or representation of knowledge such as facts, data, or opinions in any medium or form, including textual, numerical, graphic, cartographic, narrative, electronic, or audiovisual forms.
information flow control	Procedure to ensure that information transfers within a system are not made in violation of the security policy.
information resources [44 USC 3502]	Information and related resources, such as personnel, equipment, funds, and information technology.

information security
[44 USC 3552]

The protection of information and systems from unauthorized access, use, disclosure, disruption, modification, or destruction in order to provide confidentiality, integrity, and availability.

information system
[44 USC 3502]

A discrete set of information resources organized for the collection, processing, maintenance, use, sharing, dissemination, or disposition of information.

information technology
[OMB A-130]

Any services, equipment, or interconnected system(s) or subsystem(s) of equipment, that are used in the automatic acquisition, storage, analysis, evaluation, manipulation, management, movement, control, display, switching, interchange, transmission, or reception of data or information by the agency. For purposes of this definition, such services or equipment if used by the agency directly or is used by a contractor under a contract with the agency that requires its use; or to a significant extent, its use in the performance of a service or the furnishing of a product. Information technology includes computers, ancillary equipment (including imaging peripherals, input, output, and storage devices necessary for security and surveillance), peripheral equipment designed to be controlled by the central processing unit of a computer, software, firmware and similar procedures, services (including cloud computing and help-desk services or other professional services which support any point of the life cycle of the equipment or service), and related resources. Information technology does not include any equipment that is acquired by a contractor incidental to a contract which does not require its use.

insider threat

The threat that an insider will use her/his authorized access, wittingly or unwittingly, to do harm to the security of the United States. This threat can include damage to the United States through espionage, terrorism, unauthorized disclosure, or through the loss or degradation of departmental resources or capabilities.

integrity
[44 USC 3552]

Guarding against improper information modification or destruction, and includes ensuring information non-repudiation and authenticity.

internal network

A network where establishment, maintenance, and provisioning of security controls are under the direct control of organizational employees or contractors; or the cryptographic encapsulation or similar security technology implemented between organization-controlled endpoints, provides the same effect (with regard to confidentiality and integrity). An internal network is typically organization-owned, yet may be organization-controlled while not being organization-owned.

least privilege	The principle that a security architecture is designed so that each entity is granted the minimum system authorizations and resources that the entity needs to perform its function.
local access	Access to an organizational system by a user (or process acting on behalf of a user) communicating through a direct connection without the use of a network.
malicious code	Software or firmware intended to perform an unauthorized process that will have adverse impact on the confidentiality, integrity, or availability of a system. A virus, worm, Trojan horse, or other code-based entity that infects a host. Spyware and some forms of adware are also examples of malicious code.
media [FIPS 200]	Physical devices or writing surfaces including, but not limited to, magnetic tapes, optical disks, magnetic disks, Large-Scale Integration (LSI) memory chips, and printouts (but not including display media) onto which information is recorded, stored, or printed within a system.
mobile code	Software programs or parts of programs obtained from remote systems, transmitted across a network, and executed on a local system without explicit installation or execution by the recipient.
mobile device	A portable computing device that has a small form factor such that it can easily be carried by a single individual; is designed to operate without a physical connection (e.g., wirelessly transmit or receive information); possesses local, non-removable/removable data storage; and includes a self-contained power source. Mobile devices may also include voice communication capabilities, on-board sensors that allow the devices to capture information, or built-in features that synchronize local data with remote locations. Examples include smartphones, tablets, and E-readers.
multifactor authentication	Authentication using two or more different factors to achieve authentication. Factors include something you know (e.g., PIN, password); something you have (e.g., cryptographic identification device, token); or something you are (e.g., biometric). See *authenticator*.
mutual authentication [CNSSI 4009]	The process of both entities involved in a transaction verifying each other. See *bidirectional authentication*.
nonfederal organization	An entity that owns, operates, or maintains a nonfederal system.
nonfederal system	A system that does not meet the criteria for a federal system.
network	A system implemented with a collection of interconnected components. Such components may include routers, hubs, cabling, telecommunications controllers, key distribution centers, and technical control devices.

network access	Access to a system by a user (or a process acting on behalf of a user) communicating through a network (e.g., local area network, wide area network, Internet).
nonlocal maintenance	Maintenance activities conducted by individuals communicating through a network, either an external network (e.g., the Internet) or an internal network.
on behalf of (an agency) [32 CFR 2002]	A situation that occurs when: (i) a non-executive branch entity uses or operates an information system or maintains or collects information for the purpose of processing, storing, or transmitting Federal information; and (ii) those activities are not incidental to providing a service or product to the government.
organization [FIPS 200, Adapted]	An entity of any size, complexity, or positioning within an organizational structure.
personnel security [SP 800-53]	The discipline of assessing the conduct, integrity, judgment, loyalty, reliability, and stability of individuals for duties and responsibilities requiring trustworthiness.
portable storage device	A system component that can be inserted into and removed from a system, and that is used to store data or information (e.g., text, video, audio, and/or image data). Such components are typically implemented on magnetic, optical, or solid-state devices (e.g., floppy disks, compact/digital video disks, flash/thumb drives, external hard disk drives, and flash memory cards/drives that contain nonvolatile memory).
potential impact [FIPS 199]	The loss of confidentiality, integrity, or availability could be expected to have: (i) a *limited* adverse effect (FIPS Publication 199 low); (ii) a *serious* adverse effect (FIPS Publication 199 moderate); or (iii) a *severe* or *catastrophic* adverse effect (FIPS Publication 199 high) on organizational operations, organizational assets, or individuals.
privileged account	A system account with authorizations of a privileged user.
privileged user	A user that is authorized (and therefore, trusted) to perform security-relevant functions that ordinary users are not authorized to perform.
records	The recordings (automated and/or manual) of evidence of activities performed or results achieved (e.g., forms, reports, test results), which serve as a basis for verifying that the organization and the system are performing as intended. Also used to refer to units of related data fields (i.e., groups of data fields that can be accessed by a program and that contain the complete set of information on particular items).
remote access	Access to an organizational system by a user (or a process acting on behalf of a user) communicating through an external network (e.g., the Internet).

remote maintenance	Maintenance activities conducted by individuals communicating through an external network (e.g., the Internet).
replay resistance	Protection against the capture of transmitted authentication or access control information and its subsequent retransmission with the intent of producing an unauthorized effect or gaining unauthorized access.
risk [OMB A-130]	A measure of the extent to which an entity is threatened by a potential circumstance or event, and typically is a function of: (i) the adverse impact, or magnitude of harm, that would arise if the circumstance or event occurs; and (ii) the likelihood of occurrence.
risk assessment [SP 800-30]	The process of identifying risks to organizational operations (including mission, functions, image, reputation), organizational assets, individuals, other organizations, and the Nation, resulting from the operation of a system.
sanitization	Actions taken to render data written on media unrecoverable by both ordinary and, for some forms of sanitization, extraordinary means. Process to remove information from media such that data recovery is not possible. It includes removing all classified labels, markings, and activity logs.
security [CNSSI 4009]	A condition that results from the establishment and maintenance of protective measures that enable an organization to perform its mission or critical functions despite risks posed by threats to its use of systems. Protective measures may involve a combination of deterrence, avoidance, prevention, detection, recovery, and correction that should form part of the organization's risk management approach.
security assessment	See *security control assessment*.
security control [OMB A-130]	The safeguards or countermeasures prescribed for an information system or an organization to protect the confidentiality, integrity, and availability of the system and its information.
security control assessment [OMB A-130]	The testing or evaluation of security controls to determine the extent to which the controls are implemented correctly, operating as intended, and producing the desired outcome with respect to meeting the security requirements for an information system or organization.
security domain [CNSSI 4009, Adapted]	A domain that implements a security policy and is administered by a single authority.
security functions	The hardware, software, or firmware of the system responsible for enforcing the system security policy and supporting the isolation of code and data on which the protection is based.

split tunneling	The process of allowing a remote user or device to establish a non-remote connection with a system and simultaneously communicate via some other connection to a resource in an external network. This method of network access enables a user to access remote devices (e.g., a networked printer) at the same time as accessing uncontrolled networks.
system	See *information system*.
system component [SP 800-128]	A discrete identifiable information technology asset that represents a building block of a system and may include hardware, software, and firmware.
system security plan	A document that describes how an organization meets the security requirements for a system or how an organization plans to meet the requirements. In particular, the system security plan describes the system boundary; the environment in which the system operates; how the security requirements are implemented; and the relationships with or connections to other systems.
system service	A capability provided by a system that facilitates information processing, storage, or transmission.
threat [SP 800-30]	Any circumstance or event with the potential to adversely impact organizational operations, organizational assets, individuals, other organizations, or the Nation through a system via unauthorized access, destruction, disclosure, modification of information, and/or denial of service.
system user	Individual, or (system) process acting on behalf of an individual, authorized to access a system.
whitelisting	A process used to identify software programs that are authorized to execute on a system or authorized Universal Resource Locators (URL)/websites.
wireless technology	Technology that permits the transfer of information between separated points without physical connection.

APPENDIX C

ACRONYMS

COMMON ABBREVIATIONS

CERT	Computer Emergency Readiness Team
CFR	Code of Federal Regulations
CNSS	Committee on National Security Systems
CUI	Controlled Unclassified Information
DMZ	Demilitarized Zone
FAR	Federal Acquisition Requirement
FIPS	Federal Information Processing Standards
FISMA	Federal Information Security Modernization Act
IoT	Internet of Things
IP	Internet Protocol
ISO/IEC	International Organization for Standardization/International Electrotechnical Commission
ISOO	Information Security Oversight Office
IT	Information Technology
ITL	Information Technology Laboratory
NARA	National Archives and Records Administration
NFO	Nonfederal Organization
NIST	National Institute of Standards and Technology
OMB	Office of Management and Budget
SP	Special Publication
US-CERT	United States Computer Emergency Readiness Team

APPENDIX D

MAPPING TABLES

MAPPING BASIC AND DERIVED SECURITY REQUIREMENTS TO SECURITY CONTROLS

Tables D-1 through D-14 provide a mapping of the basic and derived security requirements to the security controls in [SP 800-53].[31] The mapping tables are included for informational purposes and do not impart additional security requirements beyond those requirements defined in Chapter Three. In some cases, the security controls include additional expectations beyond those required to protect CUI and have been tailored using the criteria in Chapter Two. Only the portion of the security control relevant to the security requirement is applicable. The tables also include a secondary mapping of the security controls to the relevant controls in [ISO 27001]. An asterisk (*) indicates that the ISO/IEC control does not fully satisfy the intent of the NIST control. Due to the tailoring actions carried out to develop the security requirements, satisfaction of a basic or derived requirement does *not* imply the corresponding NIST security control or control enhancement has also been satisfied, since certain elements of the control or control enhancement that are not essential to protecting the confidentiality of CUI are not reflected in those requirements.

Organizations that have implemented or plan to implement the [NIST CSF] can use the mapping of the security requirements to the security controls in [SP 800-53] and [ISO 27001] to locate the equivalent controls in the categories and subcategories associated with the core functions of the Cybersecurity Framework: identify, protect, detect, respond, and recover. The security control mapping information can be useful to organizations that wish to demonstrate compliance to the security requirements in the context of their established information security programs, when such programs have been built around the NIST or ISO/IEC security controls.

---

[31] The security controls in Tables D-1 through D-14 are taken from NIST Special Publication 800-53, Revision 4. These tables will be updated upon publication of [SP 800-53B] which will provide an update to the moderate security control baseline consistent with NIST Special Publication 800-53, Revision 5. Changes to the moderate baseline will affect future updates to the basic and derived security requirements in Chapter Three.

TABLE D-1: MAPPING ACCESS CONTROL REQUIREMENTS TO CONTROLS

SECURITY REQUIREMENTS		NIST SP 800-53 *Relevant Security Controls*		ISO/IEC 27001 *Relevant Security Controls*	
3.1 **ACCESS CONTROL**					
Basic Security Requirements					
3.1.1	Limit system access to authorized users, processes acting on behalf of authorized users, and devices (including other systems).	AC-2	Account Management	A.9.2.1	User registration and de-registration
				A.9.2.2	User access provisioning
3.1.2	Limit system access to the types of transactions and functions that authorized users are permitted to execute.			A.9.2.3	Management of privileged access rights
				A.9.2.5	Review of user access rights
				A.9.2.6	Removal or adjustment of access rights
		AC-3	Access Enforcement	A.6.2.2	Teleworking
				A.9.1.2	Access to networks and network services
				A.9.4.1	Information access restriction
				A.9.4.4	Use of privileged utility programs
				A.9.4.5	Access control to program source code
				A.13.1.1	Network controls
				A.14.1.2	Securing application services on public networks
				A.14.1.3	Protecting application services transactions
				A.18.1.3	Protection of records
		AC-17	Remote Access	A.6.2.1	Mobile device policy
				A.6.2.2	Teleworking
				A.13.1.1	Network controls
				A.13.2.1	Information transfer policies and procedures
				A.14.1.2	Securing application services on public networks
Derived Security Requirements					
3.1.3	Control the flow of CUI in accordance with approved authorizations.	AC-4	Information Flow Enforcement	A.13.1.3	Segregation in networks
				A.13.2.1	Information transfer policies and procedures

SECURITY REQUIREMENTS		NIST SP 800-53 *Relevant Security Controls*		ISO/IEC 27001 *Relevant Security Controls*	
				A.14.1.2	Securing application services on public networks
				A.14.1.3	Protecting application services transactions
3.1.4	Separate the duties of individuals to reduce the risk of malevolent activity without collusion.	AC-5	Separation of Duties	A.6.1.2	Segregation of duties
3.1.5	Employ the principle of least privilege, including for specific security functions and privileged accounts.	AC-6	Least Privilege	A.9.1.2	Access to networks and network services
				A.9.2.3	Management of privileged access rights
				A.9.4.4	Use of privileged utility programs
				A.9.4.5	Access control to program source code
		AC-6(1)	Least Privilege *Authorize Access to Security Functions*	*No direct mapping.*	
		AC-6(5)	Least Privilege *Privileged Accounts*	*No direct mapping.*	
3.1.6	Use non-privileged accounts or roles when accessing nonsecurity functions.	AC-6(2)	Least Privilege *Non-Privileged Access for Nonsecurity Functions*	*No direct mapping.*	
3.1.7	Prevent non-privileged users from executing privileged functions and capture the execution of such functions in audit logs.	AC-6(9)	Least Privilege *Log Use of Privileged Functions*	*No direct mapping.*	
		AC-6(10)	Least Privilege *Prohibit Non-Privileged Users from Executing Privileged Functions*	*No direct mapping.*	
3.1.8	Limit unsuccessful logon attempts.	AC-7	Unsuccessful Logon Attempts	A.9.4.2	Secure logon procedures
3.1.9	Provide privacy and security notices consistent with applicable CUI rules.	AC-8	System Use Notification	A.9.4.2	Secure logon procedures
3.1.10	Use session lock with pattern-hiding displays to prevent access and viewing of data after a period of inactivity.	AC-11	Session Lock	A.11.2.8	Unattended user equipment
				A.11.2.9	Clear desk and clear screen policy
		AC-11(1)	Session Lock *Pattern-Hiding Displays*	*No direct mapping.*	
3.1.11	Terminate (automatically) a user session after a defined condition.	AC-12	Session Termination	*No direct mapping.*	
3.1.12	Monitor and control remote access sessions.	AC-17(1)	Remote Access *Automated Monitoring / Control*	*No direct mapping.*	

SECURITY REQUIREMENTS		NIST SP 800-53 *Relevant Security Controls*		ISO/IEC 27001 *Relevant Security Controls*	
3.1.13	Employ cryptographic mechanisms to protect the confidentiality of remote access sessions.	AC-17(2)	Remote Access *Protection of Confidentiality / Integrity Using Encryption*	*No direct mapping.*	
3.1.14	Route remote access via managed access control points.	AC-17(3)	Remote Access *Managed Access Control Points*	*No direct mapping.*	
3.1.15	Authorize remote execution of privileged commands and remote access to security-relevant information.	AC-17(4)	Remote Access *Privileged Commands / Access*	*No direct mapping.*	
3.1.16	Authorize wireless access prior to allowing such connections.	AC-18	Wireless Access	A.6.2.1	Mobile device policy
				A.13.1.1	Network controls
				A.13.2.1	Information transfer policies and procedures
3.1.17	Protect wireless access using authentication and encryption.	AC-18(1)	Wireless Access *Authentication and Encryption*	*No direct mapping.*	
3.1.18	Control connection of mobile devices.	AC-19	Access Control for Mobile Devices	A.6.2.1	Mobile device policy
				A.11.2.6	Security of equipment and assets off-premises
				A.13.2.1	Information transfer policies and procedures
3.1.19	Encrypt CUI on mobile devices and mobile computing platforms.	AC-19(5)	Access Control for Mobile Devices *Full Device / Container-Based Encryption*	*No direct mapping.*	
3.1.20	Verify and control/limit connections to and use of external systems.	AC-20	Use of External Systems	A.11.2.6	Security of equipment and assets off-premises
				A.13.1.1	Network controls
				A.13.2.1	Information transfer policies and procedures
		AC-20(1)	Use of External Systems *Limits on Authorized Use*	*No direct mapping.*	
3.1.21	Limit use of portable storage devices on external systems.	AC-20(2)	Use of External Systems *Portable Storage Devices*	*No direct mapping.*	
3.1.22	Control CUI posted or processed on publicly accessible systems.	AC-22	Publicly Accessible Content	*No direct mapping.*	

TABLE D-2: MAPPING AWARENESS AND TRAINING REQUIREMENTS TO CONTROLS

SECURITY REQUIREMENTS		NIST SP 800-53 *Relevant Security Controls*		ISO/IEC 27001 *Relevant Security Controls*	
3.2 AWARENESS AND TRAINING					
Basic Security Requirements					
3.2.1	Ensure that managers, systems administrators, and users of organizational systems are made aware of the security risks associated with their activities and of the applicable policies, standards, and procedures related to the security of those systems.	AT-2	Security Awareness Training	A.7.2.2	Information security awareness, education, and training
				A.12.2.1	Controls against malware
		AT-3	Role-Based Security Training	A.7.2.2*	Information security awareness, education, and training
3.2.2	Ensure that personnel are trained to carry out their assigned information security-related duties and responsibilities.				
Derived Security Requirements					
3.2.3	Provide security awareness training on recognizing and reporting potential indicators of insider threat.	AT-2(2)	Security Awareness Training *Insider Threat*	*No direct mapping.*	

TABLE D-3: MAPPING AUDIT AND ACCOUNTABILITY REQUIREMENTS TO CONTROLS

SECURITY REQUIREMENTS		NIST SP 800-53 _Relevant Security Controls_		ISO/IEC 27001 _Relevant Security Controls_	
3.3 AUDIT AND ACCOUNTABILITY					
Basic Security Requirements					
3.3.1	Create and retain system audit logs and records to the extent needed to enable the monitoring, analysis, investigation, and reporting of unlawful or unauthorized system activity.	AU-2	Event Logging	_No direct mapping._	
		AU-3	Content of Audit Records	A.12.4.1*	Event logging
		AU-3(1)	Content of Audit Records _Additional Audit Information_	_No direct mapping._	
3.3.2	Ensure that the actions of individual system users can be uniquely traced to those users, so they can be held accountable for their actions.	AU-6	Audit Record Review, Analysis, and Reporting	A.12.4.1	Event logging
				A.16.1.2	Reporting information security events
				A.16.1.4	Assessment of and decision on information security events
		AU-11	Audit Record Retention	A.12.4.1	Event logging
				A.12.4.3	Administrator and operator logs
		AU-12	Audit Record Generation	A.12.4.1	Event logging
				A.16.1.7	Collection of evidence
Derived Security Requirements					
3.3.3	Review and update logged events.	AU-2(3)	Event Logging _Review and Updates_	_No direct mapping._	
3.3.4	Alert in the event of an audit logging process failure.	AU-5	Response to Audit Logging Process Failures	_No direct mapping._	
3.3.5	Correlate audit record review, analysis, and reporting processes for investigation and response to indications of unlawful, unauthorized, suspicious, or unusual activity.	AU-6(3)	Audit Record Review, Analysis, and Reporting _Correlate Audit Record Repositories_	_No direct mapping._	
3.3.6	Provide audit record reduction and report generation to support on-demand analysis and reporting.	AU-7	Audit Record Reduction and Report Generation	_No direct mapping._	
3.3.7	Provide a system capability that compares and synchronizes internal system clocks with an authoritative source to generate time stamps for audit records.	AU-8	Time Stamps	A.12.4.4	Clock synchronization
		AU-8(1)	Time Stamps _Synchronization with Authoritative Time Source_	_No direct mapping._	
3.3.8	Protect audit information and audit logging tools from	AU-9	Protection of Audit Information	A.12.4.2	Protection of log information

SECURITY REQUIREMENTS		NIST SP 800-53 *Relevant Security Controls*		ISO/IEC 27001 *Relevant Security Controls*	
	unauthorized access, modification, and deletion.			A.12.4.3	Administrator and operator logs
				A.18.1.3	Protection of records
3.3.9	Limit management of audit logging functionality to a subset of privileged users.	AU-9(4)	Protection of Audit Information *Access by Subset of Privileged Users*	*No direct mapping.*	

TABLE D-4: MAPPING CONFIGURATION MANAGEMENT REQUIREMENTS TO CONTROLS[32]

SECURITY REQUIREMENTS		NIST SP 800-53 *Relevant Security Controls*		ISO/IEC 27001 *Relevant Security Controls*	
3.4 CONFIGURATION MANAGEMENT					
Basic Security Requirements					
3.4.1	Establish and maintain baseline configurations and inventories of organizational systems (including hardware, software, firmware, and documentation) throughout the respective system development life cycles.	CM-2	Baseline Configuration	*No direct mapping.*	
		CM-6	Configuration Settings	*No direct mapping.*	
		CM-8	System Component Inventory	A.8.1.1	Inventory of assets
				A.8.1.2	Ownership of assets
		CM-8(1)	System Component Inventory *Updates During Installations / Removals*	*No direct mapping.*	
3.4.2	Establish and enforce security configuration settings for information technology products employed in organizational systems.				
Derived Security Requirements					
3.4.3	Track, review, approve or disapprove, and log changes to organizational systems.	CM-3	Configuration Change Control	A.12.1.2	Change management
				A.14.2.2	System change control procedures
				A.14.2.3	Technical review of applications after operating platform changes
				A.14.2.4	Restrictions on changes to software packages
3.4.4	Analyze the security impact of changes prior to implementation.	CM-4	Security Impact Analysis	A.14.2.3	Technical review of applications after operating platform changes
3.4.5	Define, document, approve, and enforce physical and logical access restrictions associated with changes to organizational systems.	CM-5	Access Restrictions for Change	A.9.2.3	Management of privileged access rights
				A.9.4.5	Access control to program source code
				A.12.1.2	Change management
				A.12.1.4	Separation of development, testing, and operational environments
				A.12.5.1	Installation of software on operational systems

---

[32] CM-7(5), the least functionality whitelisting policy, is listed as an alternative to CM-7(4), the least functionality blacklisting policy, for organizations desiring greater protection for systems containing CUI. CM-7(5) is only required in federal systems at the high security control baseline in accordance with NIST Special Publication 800-53.

SECURITY REQUIREMENTS		NIST SP 800-53 *Relevant Security Controls*		ISO/IEC 27001 *Relevant Security Controls*	
3.4.6	Employ the principle of least functionality by configuring organizational systems to provide only essential capabilities.	CM-7	Least Functionality	A.12.5.1*	Installation of software on operational systems
3.4.7	Restrict, disable, or prevent the use of nonessential programs, functions, ports, protocols, and services.	CM-7(1)	Least Functionality *Periodic Review*	*No direct mapping.*	
		CM-7(2)	Least Functionality *Prevent program execution*	*No direct mapping.*	
3.4.8	Apply deny-by-exception (blacklisting) policy to prevent the use of unauthorized software or deny-all, permit-by-exception (whitelisting) policy to allow the execution of authorized software.	CM-7(4)	Least Functionality *Unauthorized Software / Blacklisting*	*No direct mapping.*	
		CM-7(5)	Least Functionality *Authorized Software / Whitelisting*	*No direct mapping.*	
3.4.9	Control and monitor user-installed software.	CM-11	User-Installed Software	A.12.5.1	Installation of software on operational systems
				A.12.6.2	Restrictions on software installation

TABLE D-5: MAPPING IDENTIFICATION AND AUTHENTICATION REQUIREMENTS TO CONTROLS[33]

SECURITY REQUIREMENTS		NIST SP 800-53 *Relevant Security Controls*		ISO/IEC 27001 *Relevant Security Controls*	
3.5 IDENTIFICATION AND AUTHENTICATION					
Basic Security Requirements					
3.5.1	Identify system users, processes acting on behalf of users, and devices.	IA-2	Identification and Authentication (Organizational Users)	A.9.2.1	User registration and de-registration
3.5.2	Authenticate (or verify) the identities of users, processes, or devices, as a prerequisite to allowing access to organizational systems.	IA-3	Device Identification and Authentication	*No direct mapping.*	
		IA-5	Authenticator Management	A.9.2.1	User registration and de-registration
				A.9.2.4	Management of secret authentication information of users
				A.9.3.1	Use of secret authentication information
				A.9.4.3	Password management system
Derived Security Requirements					
3.5.3	Use multifactor authentication for local and network access to privileged accounts and for network access to non-privileged accounts.	IA-2(1)	Identification and Authentication (Organizational Users) *Network Access to Privileged Accounts*	*No direct mapping.*	
		IA-2(2)	Identification and Authentication (Organizational Users) *Network Access to Non-Privileged Accounts*	*No direct mapping.*	
		IA-2(3)	Identification and Authentication (Organizational Users) *Local Access to Privileged Accounts*	*No direct mapping.*	
3.5.4	Employ replay-resistant authentication mechanisms for network access to privileged and non-privileged accounts.	IA-2(8)	Identification and Authentication (Organizational Users) *Network Access to Privileged Accounts-Replay Resistant*	*No direct mapping.*	
		IA-2(9)	Identification and Authentication (Organizational Users) *Network Access to Non-Privileged Accounts-Replay Resistant*	*No direct mapping.*	

---

[33] IA-2(8) is *not* currently in the NIST Special Publication 800-53 moderate security control baseline although it will be added to the baseline in the next update. Employing multifactor authentication without a replay-resistant capability for non-privileged accounts creates a significant vulnerability for systems transmitting CUI.

SECURITY REQUIREMENTS		NIST SP 800-53 *Relevant Security Controls*		ISO/IEC 27001 *Relevant Security Controls*	
3.5.5	Prevent reuse of identifiers for a defined period.	IA-4	Identifier Management	A.9.2.1	User registration and de-registration
3.5.6	Disable identifiers after a defined period of inactivity.	IA-4	Identifier Management	A.9.2.1	User registration and de-registration
3.5.7	Enforce a minimum password complexity and change of characters when new passwords are created.	IA-5(1)	Authenticator Management *Password-Based Authentication*	*No direct mapping.*	
3.5.8	Prohibit password reuse for a specified number of generations.				
3.5.9	Allow temporary password use for system logons with an immediate change to a permanent password.				
3.5.10	Store and transmit only cryptographically-protected passwords.				
3.5.11	Obscure feedback of authentication information.	IA-6	Authenticator Feedback	A.9.4.2	Secure logon procedures

TABLE D-6: MAPPING INCIDENT RESPONSE REQUIREMENTS TO CONTROLS

SECURITY REQUIREMENTS		NIST SP 800-53 *Relevant Security Controls*		ISO/IEC 27001 *Relevant Security Controls*	
3.6 INCIDENT RESPONSE					
Basic Security Requirements					
3.6.1	Establish an operational incident-handling capability for organizational systems that includes preparation, detection, analysis, containment, recovery, and user response activities.	IR-2	Incident Response Training	A.7.2.2*	Information security awareness, education, and training
3.6.2	Track, document, and report incidents to designated officials and/or authorities both internal and external to the organization.	IR-4	Incident Handling	A.16.1.4	Assessment of and decision on information security events
				A.16.1.5	Response to information security incidents
				A.16.1.6	Learning from information security incidents
		IR-5	Incident Monitoring	*No direct mapping.*	
		IR-6	Incident Reporting	A.6.1.3	Contact with authorities
				A.16.1.2	Reporting information security events
		IR-7	Incident Response Assistance	*No direct mapping.*	
Derived Security Requirements					
3.6.3	Test the organizational incident response capability.	IR-3	Incident Response Testing	*No direct mapping.*	

TABLE D-7: MAPPING MAINTENANCE REQUIREMENTS TO CONTROLS

SECURITY REQUIREMENTS		NIST SP 800-53 *Relevant Security Controls*		ISO/IEC 27001 *Relevant Security Controls*	
3.7 MAINTENANCE					
Basic Security Requirements					
3.7.1	Perform maintenance on organizational systems.	MA-2	Controlled Maintenance	A.11.2.4*	Equipment maintenance
3.7.2	Provide controls on the tools, techniques, mechanisms, and personnel used to conduct system maintenance.			A.11.2.5*	Removal of assets
		MA-3	Maintenance Tools	*No direct mapping.*	
		MA-3(1)	Maintenance Tools *Inspect Tools*	*No direct mapping.*	
		MA-3(2)	Maintenance Tools *Inspect Media*	*No direct mapping.*	
Derived Security Requirements					
3.7.3	Ensure equipment removed for off-site maintenance is sanitized of any CUI.	MA-2	Controlled Maintenance	A.11.2.4*	Equipment maintenance
				A.11.2.5*	Removal of assets
3.7.4	Check media containing diagnostic and test programs for malicious code before the media are used in organizational systems.	MA-3(2)	Maintenance Tools *Inspect Media*	*No direct mapping.*	
3.7.5	Require multifactor authentication to establish nonlocal maintenance sessions via external network connections and terminate such connections when nonlocal maintenance is complete.	MA-4	Nonlocal Maintenance	*No direct mapping.*	
3.7.6	Supervise the maintenance activities of maintenance personnel without required access authorization.	MA-5	Maintenance Personnel	*No direct mapping.*	

TABLE D-8: MAPPING MEDIA PROTECTION REQUIREMENTS TO CONTROLS[34]

SECURITY REQUIREMENTS		NIST SP 800-53 *Relevant Security Controls*		ISO/IEC 27001 *Relevant Security Controls*	
3.8 MEDIA PROTECTION					
Basic Security Requirements					
3.8.1	Protect (i.e., physically control and securely store) system media containing CUI, both paper and digital.	MP-2	Media Access	A.8.2.3	Handling of Assets
				A.8.3.1	Management of removable media
				A.11.2.9	Clear desk and clear screen policy
3.8.2	Limit access to CUI on system media to authorized users.	MP-4	Media Storage	A.8.2.3	Handling of Assets
				A.8.3.1	Management of removable media
3.8.3	Sanitize or destroy system media containing CUI before disposal or release for reuse.			A.11.2.9	Clear desk and clear screen policy
		MP-6	Media Sanitization	A.8.2.3	Handling of Assets
				A.8.3.1	Management of removable media
				A.8.3.2	Disposal of media
				A.11.2.7	Secure disposal or reuse of equipment
Derived Security Requirements					
3.8.4	Mark media with necessary CUI markings and distribution limitations.	MP-3	Media Marking	A.8.2.2	Labelling of Information
3.8.5	Control access to media containing CUI and maintain accountability for media during transport outside of controlled areas.	MP-5	Media Transport	A.8.2.3	Handling of Assets
				A.8.3.1	Management of removable media
				A.8.3.3	Physical media transfer
				A.11.2.5	Removal of assets
				A.11.2.6	Security of equipment and assets off-premises
3.8.6	Implement cryptographic mechanisms to protect the confidentiality of CUI stored on digital media during transport unless otherwise protected by alternative physical safeguards.	MP-5(4)	Media Transport *Cryptographic Protection*	No direct mapping.	
3.8.7	Control the use of removable media on system components.	MP-7	Media Use	A.8.2.3	Handling of Assets
				A.8.3.1	Management of removable media

---

[34] CP-9, *Information System Backup*, is included with the Media Protection family since the Contingency Planning family was not included in the security requirements.

SECURITY REQUIREMENTS	NIST SP 800-53 _Relevant Security Controls_		ISO/IEC 27001 _Relevant Security Controls_	
3.8.8 Prohibit the use of portable storage devices when such devices have no identifiable owner.	MP-7(1)	Media Use _Prohibit Use Without Owner_	_No direct mapping._	
3.8.9 Protect the confidentiality of backup CUI at storage locations.	CP-9	System Backup	A.12.3.1	Information backup
			A.17.1.2	Implementing information security continuity
			A.18.1.3	Protection of records

TABLE D-9: MAPPING PERSONNEL SECURITY REQUIREMENTS TO CONTROLS

SECURITY REQUIREMENTS		NIST SP 800-53 *Relevant Security Controls*		ISO/IEC 27001 *Relevant Security Controls*	
3.9 PERSONNEL SECURITY					
Basic Security Requirements					
3.9.1	Screen individuals prior to authorizing access to organizational systems containing CUI.	PS-3	Personnel Screening	A.7.1.1	Screening
		PS-4	Personnel Termination	A.7.3.1	Termination or change of employment responsibilities
3.9.2	Ensure that organizational systems containing CUI are protected during and after personnel actions such as terminations and transfers.			A.8.1.4	Return of assets
		PS-5	Personnel Transfer	A.7.3.1	Termination or change of employment responsibilities
				A.8.1.4	Return of assets
Derived Security Requirements		None.			

SECURITY REQUIREMENTS	NIST SP 800-53 *Relevant Security Controls*		ISO/IEC 27001 *Relevant Security Controls*	
3.10 PHYSICAL PROTECTION				
Basic Security Requirements				
3.10.1 Limit physical access to organizational systems, equipment, and the respective operating environments to authorized individuals.	PE-2	Physical Access Authorizations	A.11.1.2*	Physical entry controls
	PE-4	Access Control for Transmission Medium	A.11.1.2	Physical entry controls
			A.11.2.3	Cabling security
	PE-5	Access Control for Output Devices	A.11.1.2	Physical entry controls
3.10.2 Protect and monitor the physical facility and support infrastructure for organizational systems.			A.11.1.3	Securing offices, rooms, and facilities
	PE-6	Monitoring Physical Access	*No direct mapping.*	
Derived Security Requirements				
3.10.3 Escort visitors and monitor visitor activity.	PE-3	Physical Access Control	A.11.1.1	Physical security perimeter
			A.11.1.2	Physical entry controls
3.10.4 Maintain audit logs of physical access.			A.11.1.3	Securing offices, rooms, and facilities
3.10.5 Control and manage physical access devices.				
3.10.6 Enforce safeguarding measures for CUI at alternate work sites.	PE-17	Alternate Work Site	A.6.2.2	Teleworking
			A.11.2.6	Security of equipment and assets off-premises
			A.13.2.1	Information transfer policies and procedures

TABLE D-11: MAPPING RISK ASSESSMENT REQUIREMENTS TO CONTROLS

SECURITY REQUIREMENTS	NIST SP 800-53 *Relevant Security Controls*		ISO/IEC 27001 *Relevant Security Controls*	
3.11 RISK ASSESSMENT				
Basic Security Requirements				
3.11.1 Periodically assess the risk to organizational operations (including mission, functions, image, or reputation), organizational assets, and individuals, resulting from the operation of organizational systems and the associated processing, storage, or transmission of CUI.	RA-3	Risk Assessment	A.12.6.1*	Management of technical vulnerabilities
Derived Security Requirements				
3.11.2 Scan for vulnerabilities in organizational systems and applications periodically and when new vulnerabilities affecting those systems and applications are identified.	RA-5	Vulnerability Scanning	A.12.6.1*	Management of technical vulnerabilities
	RA-5(5)	Vulnerability Scanning *Privileged Access*	*No direct mapping.*	
3.11.3 Remediate vulnerabilities in accordance with risk assessments.	RA-5	Vulnerability Scanning	A.12.6.1*	Management of technical vulnerabilities

TABLE D-12: MAPPING SECURITY ASSESSMENT REQUIREMENTS TO CONTROLS

SECURITY REQUIREMENTS	NIST SP 800-53 *Relevant Security Controls*		ISO/IEC 27001 *Relevant Security Controls*	
3.12 SECURITY ASSESSMENT				
Basic Security Requirements				
3.12.1 Periodically assess the security controls in organizational systems to determine if the controls are effective in their application.	CA-2	Security Assessments	A.14.2.8	System security testing
			A.18.2.2	Compliance with security policies and standards
			A.18.2.3	Technical compliance review
3.12.2 Develop and implement plans of action designed to correct deficiencies and reduce or eliminate vulnerabilities in organizational systems.	CA-5	Plan of Action and Milestones	*No direct mapping.*	
	CA-7	Continuous Monitoring	*No direct mapping.*	
3.12.3 Monitor security controls on an ongoing basis to ensure the continued effectiveness of the controls.	PL-2	System Security Plan	A.6.1.2	Information security coordination
3.12.4 Develop, document, and periodically update system security plans that describe system boundaries, system environments of operation, how security requirements are implemented, and the relationships with or connections to other systems.				
Derived Security Requirements	None.			

TABLE D-13:　MAPPING SYSTEM AND COMMUNICATIONS PROTECTION REQUIREMENTS TO CONTROLS[35]

SECURITY REQUIREMENTS	NIST SP 800-53 *Relevant Security Controls*		ISO/IEC 27001 *Relevant Security Controls*	
3.13　SYSTEM AND COMMUNICATIONS PROTECTION				
Basic Security Requirements				
3.13.1　Monitor, control, and protect communications (i.e., information transmitted or received by organizational systems) at the external boundaries and key internal boundaries of organizational systems.	SC-7	Boundary Protection	A.13.1.1	Network controls
			A.13.1.3	Segregation in networks
			A.13.2.1	Information transfer policies and procedures
			A.14.1.3	Protecting application services transactions
3.13.2　Employ architectural designs, software development techniques, and systems engineering principles that promote effective information security within organizational systems.	SA-8	Security Engineering Principles	A.14.2.5	Secure system engineering principles
Derived Security Requirements				
3.13.3　Separate user functionality from system management functionality.	SC-2	Application Partitioning	*No direct mapping.*	
3.13.4　Prevent unauthorized and unintended information transfer via shared system resources.	SC-4	Information in Shared Resources	*No direct mapping.*	
3.13.5　Implement subnetworks for publicly accessible system components that are physically or logically separated from internal networks.	SC-7	Boundary Protection	A.13.1.1	Network controls
			A.13.1.3	Segregation in networks
			A.13.2.1	Information transfer policies and procedures
			A.14.1.3	Protecting application services transactions
3.13.6　Deny network communications traffic by default and allow network communications traffic by exception (i.e., deny all, permit by exception).	SC-7(5)	Boundary Protection *Deny by Default / Allow by Exception*	*No direct mapping.*	

---

[35] SA-8, *Security Engineering Principles*, is included with the System and Communications Protection family since the System and Services Acquisition family was not included in the security requirements.

SECURITY REQUIREMENTS		NIST SP 800-53 *Relevant Security Controls*		ISO/IEC 27001 *Relevant Security Controls*	
3.13.7	Prevent remote devices from simultaneously establishing non-remote connections with organizational systems and communicating via some other connection to resources in external networks (i.e., split tunneling).	SC-7(7)	Boundary Protection *Prevent Split Tunneling for Remote Devices*	No direct mapping.	
3.13.8	Implement cryptographic mechanisms to prevent unauthorized disclosure of CUI during transmission unless otherwise protected by alternative physical safeguards.	SC-8	Transmission Confidentiality and Integrity	A.8.2.3	Handling of Assets
				A.13.1.1	Network controls
				A.13.2.1	Information transfer policies and procedures
				A.13.2.3	Electronic messaging
				A.14.1.2	Securing application services on public networks
				A.14.1.3	Protecting application services transactions
		SC-8(1)	Transmission Confidentiality and Integrity *Cryptographic or Alternate Physical Protection*	No direct mapping.	
3.13.9	Terminate network connections associated with communications sessions at the end of the sessions or after a defined period of inactivity.	SC-10	Network Disconnect	A.13.1.1	Network controls
3.13.10	Establish and manage cryptographic keys for cryptography employed in organizational systems.	SC-12	Cryptographic Key Establishment and Management	A.10.1.2	Key Management
3.13.11	Employ FIPS-validated cryptography when used to protect the confidentiality of CUI.	SC-13	Cryptographic Protection	A.10.1.1	Policy on the use of cryptographic controls
				A.14.1.2	Securing application services on public networks
				A.14.1.3	Protecting application services transactions
				A.18.1.5	Regulation of cryptographic controls
3.13.12	Prohibit remote activation of collaborative computing devices and provide indication of devices in use to users present at the device.	SC-15	Collaborative Computing Devices	A.13.2.1*	Information transfer policies and procedures
3.13.13	Control and monitor the use of mobile code.	SC-18	Mobile Code	No direct mapping.	

SECURITY REQUIREMENTS		NIST SP 800-53 *Relevant Security Controls*		ISO/IEC 27001 *Relevant Security Controls*	
3.13.14	Control and monitor the use of Voice over Internet Protocol (VoIP) technologies.	SC-19	Voice over Internet Protocol	*No direct mapping.*	
3.13.15	Protect the authenticity of communications sessions.	SC-23	Session Authenticity	*No direct mapping.*	
3.13.16	Protect the confidentiality of CUI at rest.	SC-28	Protection of Information at Rest	A.8.2.3*	Handling of Assets

TABLE D-14: MAPPING SYSTEM AND INFORMATION INTEGRITY REQUIREMENTS TO CONTROLS

SECURITY REQUIREMENTS	NIST SP 800-53 *Relevant Security Controls*		ISO/IEC 27001 *Relevant Security Controls*	
3.14 SYSTEM AND INFORMATION INTEGRITY				
Basic Security Requirements				
3.14.1 Identify, report, and correct system flaws in a timely manner.	SI-2	Flaw Remediation	A.12.6.1	Management of technical vulnerabilities
3.14.2 Provide protection from malicious code at designated locations within organizational systems.			A.14.2.2	System change control procedures
			A.14.2.3	Technical review of applications after operating platform changes
3.14.3 Monitor system security alerts and advisories and take action in response.			A.16.1.3	Reporting information security weaknesses
	SI-3	Malicious Code Protection	A.12.2.1	Controls against malware
	SI-5	Security Alerts, Advisories, and Directives	A.6.1.4*	Contact with special interest groups
Derived Security Requirements				
3.14.4 Update malicious code protection mechanisms when new releases are available.	SI-3	Malicious Code Protection	A.12.2.1	Controls against malware
3.14.5 Perform periodic scans of organizational systems and real-time scans of files from external sources as files are downloaded, opened, or executed.				
3.14.6 Monitor organizational systems, including inbound and outbound communications traffic, to detect attacks and indicators of potential attacks.	SI-4	System Monitoring	*No direct mapping.*	
	SI-4(4)	System Monitoring *Inbound and Outbound Communications Traffic*	*No direct mapping.*	
3.14.7 Identify unauthorized use of organizational systems.	SI-4	System Monitoring	*No direct mapping.*	

APPENDIX E

TAILORING CRITERIA
LISTING OF MODERATE SECURITY CONTROL BASELINE AND TAILORING ACTIONS

This appendix provides a list of the security controls in the [SP 800-53][36] moderate baseline, one of the sources along with [FIPS 200], used to develop the CUI security requirements described in Chapter Three. Tables E-1 through E-17 contain the specific tailoring actions that have been carried out on the controls in accordance with the tailoring criteria established by NIST and NARA. The tailoring actions facilitated the development of the CUI derived security requirements which supplement the basic security requirements.[37] There are three primary criteria for eliminating a security control or control enhancement from the moderate baseline including—

- The control or control enhancement is uniquely federal (i.e., primarily the responsibility of the federal government);

- The control or control enhancement is not directly related to protecting the confidentiality of CUI;[38] or

- The control or control enhancement is expected to be routinely satisfied by nonfederal organizations without specification.[39]

The following symbols in Table E are used in Tables E-1 through E-17 to specify the tailoring actions taken or when no tailoring actions were required.

TABLE E: TAILORING ACTION SYMBOLS

TAILORING SYMBOL	TAILORING CRITERIA
NCO	NOT DIRECTLY RELATED TO PROTECTING THE CONFIDENTIALITY OF CUI.
FED	UNIQUELY FEDERAL, PRIMARILY THE RESPONSIBILITY OF THE FEDERAL GOVERNMENT.
NFO	EXPECTED TO BE ROUTINELY SATISFIED BY NONFEDERAL ORGANIZATIONS WITHOUT SPECIFICATION.
CUI	THE CUI BASIC OR DERIVED SECURITY REQUIREMENT IS REFLECTED IN AND IS TRACEABLE TO THE SECURITY CONTROL, CONTROL ENHANCEMENT, OR SPECIFIC ELEMENTS OF THE CONTROL/ENHANCEMENT.

---

[36] The security controls in Tables E-1 through E-14 are taken from NIST Special Publication 800-53, Revision 4. These tables will be updated upon publication of [SP 800-53B] which will provide an update to the moderate security control baseline consistent with NIST Special Publication 800-53, Revision 5. Changes to the moderate baseline will affect future updates to the basic and derived security requirements in Chapter Three.

[37] The same *tailoring criteria* were applied to the security requirements in [FIPS 200] resulting in the CUI basic security requirements described in Chapter Three.

[38] While the primary purpose of this publication is to define requirements to protect the confidentiality of CUI, there is a close relationship between the security objectives of confidentiality and integrity. Therefore, the security controls in the [SP 800-53] moderate baseline that support protection against unauthorized disclosure also support protection against unauthorized modification.

[39] The security controls tailored out of the moderate baseline (i.e., controls specifically marked as either NCO or NFO in Tables E-1 through E-17), are often included as part of an organization's comprehensive security program.

TABLE E-1: TAILORING ACTIONS FOR ACCESS CONTROLS

NIST SP 800-53 MODERATE BASELINE SECURITY CONTROLS		TAILORING ACTION
AC-1	Access Control Policy and Procedures	NFO
AC-2	Account Management	CUI
AC-2(1)	*ACCOUNT MANAGEMENT │ AUTOMATED SYSTEM ACCOUNT MANAGEMENT*	NCO
AC-2(2)	*ACCOUNT MANAGEMENT │ REMOVAL OF TEMPORARY / EMERGENCY ACCOUNTS*	NCO
AC-2(3)	*ACCOUNT MANAGEMENT │ DISABLE INACTIVE ACCOUNTS*	NCO
AC-2(4)	*ACCOUNT MANAGEMENT │ AUTOMATED AUDIT ACTIONS*	NCO
AC-3	Access Enforcement	CUI
AC-4	Information Flow Enforcement	CUI
AC-5	Separation of Duties	CUI
AC-6	Least Privilege	CUI
AC-6(1)	*LEAST PRIVILEGE │ AUTHORIZE ACCESS TO SECURITY FUNCTIONS*	CUI
AC-6(2)	*LEAST PRIVILEGE │ NON-PRIVILEGED ACCESS FOR NONSECURITY FUNCTIONS*	CUI
AC-6(5)	*LEAST PRIVILEGE │ PRIVILEGED ACCOUNTS*	CUI
AC-6(9)	*LEAST PRIVILEGE │ AUDITING USE OF PRIVILEGED FUNCTIONS*	CUI
AC-6(10)	*LEAST PRIVILEGE │ PROHIBIT NON-PRIVILEGED USERS FROM EXECUTING PRIVILEGED FUNCTIONS*	CUI
AC-7	Unsuccessful Logon Attempts	CUI
AC-8	System Use Notification	CUI
AC-11	Session Lock	CUI
AC-11(1)	*SESSION LOCK │ PATTERN-HIDING DISPLAYS*	CUI
AC-12	Session Termination	CUI
AC-14	Permitted Actions without Identification or Authentication	FED
AC-17	Remote Access	CUI
AC-17(1)	*REMOTE ACCESS │ AUTOMATED MONITORING / CONTROL*	CUI
AC-17(2)	*REMOTE ACCESS │ PROTECTION OF CONFIDENTIALITY / INTEGRITY USING ENCRYPTION*	CUI
AC-17(3)	*REMOTE ACCESS │ MANAGED ACCESS CONTROL POINTS*	CUI
AC-17(4)	*REMOTE ACCESS │ PRIVILEGED COMMANDS / ACCESS*	CUI
AC-18	Wireless Access	CUI
AC-18(1)	*WIRELESS ACCESS │ AUTHENTICATION AND ENCRYPTION*	CUI
AC-19	Access Control for Mobile Devices	CUI
AC-19(5)	*ACCESS CONTROL FOR MOBILE DEVICES │ FULL DEVICE / CONTAINER-BASED ENCRYPTION*	CUI
AC-20	Use of External Systems	CUI
AC-20(1)	*USE OF EXTERNAL SYSTEMS │ LIMITS ON AUTHORIZED USE*	CUI
AC-20(2)	*USE OF EXTERNAL SYSTEMS │ PORTABLE STORAGE DEVICES*	CUI
AC-21	Information Sharing	FED
AC-22	Publicly Accessible Content	CUI

TABLE E-2: TAILORING ACTIONS FOR AWARENESS AND TRAINING CONTROLS

NIST SP 800-53 MODERATE BASELINE SECURITY CONTROLS		TAILORING ACTION
AT-1	Security Awareness and Training Policy and Procedures	NFO
AT-2	Security Awareness Training	CUI
AT-2(2)	*SECURITY AWARENESS | INSIDER THREAT*	CUI
AT-3	Role-Based Security Training	CUI
AT-4	Security Training Records	NFO

TABLE E-3: TAILORING ACTIONS FOR AUDIT AND ACCOUNTABILITY CONTROLS

	NIST SP 800-53 MODERATE BASELINE SECURITY CONTROLS	TAILORING ACTION
AU-1	Audit and Accountability Policy and Procedures	NFO
AU-2	Audit Events	CUI
AU-2(3)	*AUDIT EVENTS | REVIEWS AND UPDATES*	CUI
AU-3	Content of Audit Records	CUI
AU-3(1)	*CONTENT OF AUDIT RECORDS | ADDITIONAL AUDIT INFORMATION*	CUI
AU-4	Audit Storage Capacity	NCO
AU-5	Response to Audit Logging Process Failures	CUI
AU-6	Audit Review, Analysis, and Reporting	CUI
AU-6(1)	*AUDIT REVIEW, ANALYSIS, AND REPORTING | PROCESS INTEGRATION*	NCO
AU-6(3)	*AUDIT REVIEW, ANALYSIS, AND REPORTING | CORRELATE AUDIT REPOSITORIES*	CUI
AU-7	Audit Reduction and Report Generation	CUI
AU-7(1)	*AUDIT REDUCTION AND REPORT GENERATION | AUTOMATIC PROCESSING*	NCO
AU-8	Time Stamps	CUI
AU-8(1)	*TIME STAMPS | SYNCHRONIZATION WITH AUTHORITATIVE TIME SOURCE*	CUI
AU-9	Protection of Audit Information	CUI
AU-9(4)	*PROTECTION OF AUDIT INFORMATION | ACCESS BY SUBSET OF PRIVILEGED USERS*	CUI
AU-11	Audit Record Retention	NCO
AU-12	Audit Generation	CUI

TABLE E-4: TAILORING ACTIONS FOR SECURITY ASSESSMENT AND AUTHORIZATION CONTROLS

	NIST SP 800-53 MODERATE BASELINE SECURITY CONTROLS	TAILORING ACTION
CA-1	Security Assessment and Authorization Policies and Procedures	NFO
CA-2	Security Assessments	CUI
CA-2(1)	*SECURITY ASSESSMENTS | INDEPENDENT ASSESSORS*	NFO
CA-3	System Interconnections	NFO
CA-3(5)	*SYSTEM INTERCONNECTIONS | RESTRICTIONS ON EXTERNAL SYSTEM CONNECTIONS*	NFO
CA-5	Plan of Action and Milestones	CUI
CA-6	Security Authorization	FED
CA-7	Continuous Monitoring	CUI
CA-7(1)	*CONTINUOUS MONITORING | INDEPENDENT ASSESSMENT*	NFO
CA-9	Internal System Connections	NFO

TABLE E-5: TAILORING ACTIONS FOR CONFIGURATION MANAGEMENT CONTROLS[40]

	NIST SP 800-53 MODERATE BASELINE SECURITY CONTROLS	TAILORING ACTION
CM-1	Configuration Management Policy and Procedures	NFO
CM-2	Baseline Configuration	CUI
CM-2(1)	*BASELINE CONFIGURATION │ REVIEWS AND UPDATES*	NFO
CM-2(3)	*BASELINE CONFIGURATION │ RETENTION OF PREVIOUS CONFIGURATIONS*	NCO
CM-2(7)	*BASELINE CONFIGURATION │ CONFIGURE SYSTEMS, COMPONENTS, OR DEVICES FOR HIGH-RISK AREAS*	NFO
CM-3	Configuration Change Control	CUI
CM-3(2)	*CONFIGURATION CHANGE CONTROL │ TEST / VALIDATE / DOCUMENT CHANGES*	NFO
CM-4	Security Impact Analysis	CUI
CM-5	Access Restrictions for Change	CUI
CM-6	Configuration Settings	CUI
CM-7	Least Functionality	CUI
CM-7(1)	*LEAST FUNCTIONALITY │ PERIODIC REVIEW*	CUI
CM-7(2)	*LEAST FUNCTIONALITY │ PREVENT PROGRAM EXECUTION*	CUI
CM-7(4)(5)	*LEAST FUNCTIONALITY │ UNAUTHORIZED OR AUTHORIZED SOFTWARE / BLACKLISTING OR WHITELISTING*	CUI
CM-8	System Component Inventory	CUI
CM-8(1)	*SYSTEM COMPONENT INVENTORY │ UPDATES DURING INSTALLATIONS / REMOVALS*	CUI
CM-8(3)	*SYSTEM COMPONENT INVENTORY │ AUTOMATED UNAUTHORIZED COMPONENT DETECTION*	NCO
CM-8(5)	*SYSTEM COMPONENT INVENTORY │ NO DUPLICATE ACCOUNTING OF COMPONENTS*	NFO
CM-9	Configuration Management Plan	NFO
CM-10	Software Usage Restrictions	NCO
CM-11	User-Installed Software	CUI

---

[40] CM-7(5), Least Functionality *whitelisting*, is not in the moderate security control baseline in accordance with NIST Special Publication 800-53. However, it is offered as an optional and stronger policy alternative to *blacklisting*.

TABLE E-6: TAILORING ACTIONS FOR CONTINGENCY PLANNING CONTROLS[41]

	NIST SP 800-53 MODERATE BASELINE SECURITY CONTROLS	TAILORING ACTION
CP-1	Contingency Planning Policy and Procedures	NCO
CP-2	Contingency Plan	NCO
CP-2(1)	*CONTINGENCY PLAN │ COORDINATE WITH RELATED PLANS*	NCO
CP-2(3)	*CONTINGENCY PLAN │ RESUME ESSENTIAL MISSIONS / BUSINESS FUNCTIONS*	NCO
CP-2(8)	*CONTINGENCY PLAN │ IDENTIFY CRITICAL ASSETS*	NCO
CP-3	Contingency Training	NCO
CP-4	Contingency Plan Testing	NCO
CP-4(1)	*CONTINGENCY PLAN TESTING │ COORDINATE WITH RELATED PLANS*	NCO
CP-6	Alternate Storage Site	NCO
CP-6(1)	*ALTERNATE STORAGE SITE │ SEPARATION FROM PRIMARY SITE*	NCO
CP-6(3)	*ALTERNATE STORAGE SITE │ ACCESSIBILITY*	NCO
CP-7	Alternate Processing Site	NCO
CP-7(1)	*ALTERNATE PROCESSING SITE │ SEPARATION FROM PRIMARY SITE*	NCO
CP-7(2)	*ALTERNATE PROCESSING SITE │ ACCESSIBILITY*	NCO
CP-7(3)	*ALTERNATE PROCESSING SITE │ PRIORITY OF SERVICE*	NCO
CP-8	Telecommunications Services	NCO
CP-8(1)	*TELECOMMUNICATIONS SERVICES │ PRIORITY OF SERVICE PROVISIONS*	NCO
CP-8(2)	*TELECOMMUNICATIONS SERVICES │ SINGLE POINTS OF FAILURE*	NCO
CP-9	System Backup	CUI
CP-9(1)	*SYSTEM BACKUP │ TESTING FOR RELIABILITY / INTEGRITY*	NCO
CP-10	System Recovery and Reconstitution	NCO
CP-10(2)	*SYSTEM RECOVERY AND RECONSTITUTION │ TRANSACTION RECOVERY*	NCO

---

[41] CP-9 is grouped with the security controls in the *Media Protection* family in Appendix D since the *Contingency Planning* family was not included in the security requirements.

TABLE E-7: TAILORING ACTIONS FOR IDENTIFICATION AND AUTHENTICATION CONTROLS

	NIST SP 800-53 MODERATE BASELINE SECURITY CONTROLS	TAILORING ACTION
IA-1	Identification and Authentication Policy and Procedures	NFO
IA-2	Identification and Authentication (Organizational Users)	CUI
IA-2(1)	*IDENTIFICATION AND AUTHENTICATION (ORGANIZATIONAL USERS) | NETWORK ACCESS TO PRIVILEGED ACCOUNTS*	CUI
IA-2(2)	*IDENTIFICATION AND AUTHENTICATION (ORGANIZATIONAL USERS) | NETWORK ACCESS TO NON-PRIVILEGED ACCOUNTS*	CUI
IA-2(3)	*IDENTIFICATION AND AUTHENTICATION (ORGANIZATIONAL USERS) | LOCAL ACCESS TO PRIVILEGED ACCOUNTS*	CUI
IA-2(8)	*IDENTIFICATION AND AUTHENTICATION (ORGANIZATIONAL USERS) | NETWORK ACCESS TO PRIVILEGED ACCOUNTS - REPLAY RESISTANT*	CUI
IA-2(9)	*IDENTIFICATION AND AUTHENTICATION (ORGANIZATIONAL USERS) | NETWORK ACCESS TO NON-PRIVILEGED ACCOUNTS - REPLAY RESISTANT*	CUI
IA-2(11)	*IDENTIFICATION AND AUTHENTICATION (ORGANIZATIONAL USERS) | REMOTE ACCESS - SEPARATE DEVICE*	FED
IA-2(12)	*IDENTIFICATION AND AUTHENTICATION (ORGANIZATIONAL USERS) | ACCEPTANCE OF PIV CREDENTIALS*	FED
IA-3	Device Identification and Authentication	CUI
IA-4	Identifier Management	CUI
IA-5	Authenticator Management	CUI
IA-5(1)	*AUTHENTICATOR MANAGEMENT | PASSWORD-BASED AUTHENTICATION*	CUI
IA-5(2)	*AUTHENTICATOR MANAGEMENT | PKI-BASED AUTHENTICATION*	FED
IA-5(3)	*AUTHENTICATOR MANAGEMENT | IN-PERSON OR TRUSTED THIRD-PARTY REGISTRATION*	FED
IA-5(11)	*AUTHENTICATOR MANAGEMENT | HARDWARE TOKEN-BASED AUTHENTICATION*	FED
IA-6	Authenticator Feedback	CUI
IA-7	Cryptographic Module Authentication	FED
IA-8	Identification and Authentication (Non-Organizational Users)	FED
IA-8(1)	*IDENTIFICATION AND AUTHENTICATION (NON-ORGANIZATIONAL USERS) | ACCEPTANCE OF PIV CREDENTIALS FROM OTHER AGENCIES*	FED
IA-8(2)	*IDENTIFICATION AND AUTHENTICATION (NON-ORGANIZATIONAL USERS) | ACCEPTANCE OF THIRD-PARTY CREDENTIALS*	FED
IA-8(3)	*IDENTIFICATION AND AUTHENTICATION (NON-ORGANIZATIONAL USERS) | USE OF FICAM-APPROVED PRODUCTS*	FED
IA-8(4)	*IDENTIFICATION AND AUTHENTICATION (NON-ORGANIZATIONAL USERS) | USE OF FICAM-ISSUED PROFILES*	FED

TABLE E-8: TAILORING ACTIONS FOR INCIDENT RESPONSE CONTROLS

NIST SP 800-53 MODERATE BASELINE SECURITY CONTROLS		TAILORING ACTION
IR-1	Incident Response Policy and Procedures	NFO
IR-2	Incident Response Training	CUI
IR-3	Incident Response Testing	CUI
IR-3(2)	*INCIDENT RESPONSE TESTING	COORDINATION WITH RELATED PLANS*	NCO
IR-4	Incident Handling	CUI
IR-4(1)	*INCIDENT HANDLING	AUTOMATED INCIDENT HANDLING PROCESSES*	NCO
IR-5	Incident Monitoring	CUI
IR-6	Incident Reporting	CUI
IR-6(1)	*INCIDENT REPORTING	AUTOMATED REPORTING*	NCO
IR-7	Incident Response Assistance	CUI
IR-7(1)	*INCIDENT RESPONSE ASSISTANCE	AUTOMATION SUPPORT FOR AVAILABILITY OF INFORMATION / SUPPORT*	NCO
IR-8	Incident Response Plan	NFO

TABLE E-9: TAILORING ACTIONS FOR MAINTENANCE CONTROLS

NIST SP 800-53 MODERATE BASELINE SECURITY CONTROLS		TAILORING ACTION
MA-1	System Maintenance Policy and Procedures	NFO
MA-2	Controlled Maintenance	CUI
MA-3	Maintenance Tools	CUI
MA-3(1)	*MAINTENANCE TOOLS	INSPECT TOOLS*	CUI
MA-3(2)	*MAINTENANCE TOOLS	INSPECT MEDIA*	CUI
MA-4	Nonlocal Maintenance	CUI
MA-4(2)	*NONLOCAL MAINTENANCE	DOCUMENT NONLOCAL MAINTENANCE*	NFO
MA-5	Maintenance Personnel	CUI
MA-6	Timely Maintenance	NCO

TABLE E-10: TAILORING ACTIONS FOR MEDIA PROTECTION CONTROLS

	NIST SP 800-53 MODERATE BASELINE SECURITY CONTROLS	TAILORING ACTION
MP-1	Media Protection Policy and Procedures	NFO
MP-2	Media Access	CUI
MP-3	Media Marking	CUI
MP-4	Media Storage	CUI
MP-5	Media Transport	CUI
MP-5(4)	*MEDIA TRANSPORT	CRYPTOGRAPHIC PROTECTION*	CUI
MP-6	Media Sanitization	CUI
MP-7	Media Use	CUI
MP-7(1)	*MEDIA USE	PROHIBIT USE WITHOUT OWNER*	CUI

TABLE E-11: TAILORING ACTIONS FOR PHYSICAL AND ENVIRONMENTAL PROTECTION CONTROLS

	NIST SP 800-53 MODERATE BASELINE SECURITY CONTROLS	TAILORING ACTION
PE-1	Physical and Environmental Protection Policy and Procedures	NFO
PE-2	Physical Access Authorizations	CUI
PE-3	Physical Access Control	CUI
PE-4	Access Control for Transmission Medium	CUI
PE-5	Access Control for Output Devices	CUI
PE-6	Monitoring Physical Access	CUI
PE-6(1)	*MONITORING PHYSICAL ACCESS	INTRUSION ALARMS / SURVEILLANCE EQUIPMENT*	NFO
PE-8	Visitor Access Records	NFO
PE-9	Power Equipment and Cabling	NCO
PE-10	Emergency Shutoff	NCO
PE-11	Emergency Power	NCO
PE-12	Emergency Lighting	NCO
PE-13	Fire Protection	NCO
PE-13(3)	*FIRE PROTECTION	AUTOMATIC FIRE SUPPRESSION*	NCO
PE-14	Temperature and Humidity Controls	NCO
PE-15	Water Damage Protection	NCO
PE-16	Delivery and Removal	NFO
PE-17	Alternate Work Site	CUI

TABLE E-12: TAILORING ACTIONS FOR PLANNING CONTROLS

NIST SP 800-53 MODERATE BASELINE SECURITY CONTROLS		TAILORING ACTION
PL-1	Security Planning Policy and Procedures	NFO
PL-2	System Security Plan	CUI
PL-2(3)	*SYSTEM SECURITY PLAN	PLAN / COORDINATE WITH OTHER ORGANIZATIONAL ENTITIES*	NFO
PL-4	Rules of Behavior	NFO
PL-4(1)	*RULES OF BEHAVIOR	SOCIAL MEDIA AND NETWORKING RESTRICTIONS*	NFO
PL-8	Information Security Architecture	NFO

TABLE E-13: TAILORING ACTIONS FOR PERSONNEL SECURITY CONTROLS

NIST SP 800-53 MODERATE BASELINE SECURITY CONTROLS		TAILORING ACTION
PS-1	Personnel Security Policy and Procedures	NFO
PS-2	Position Risk Designation	FED
PS-3	Personnel Screening	CUI
PS-4	Personnel Termination	CUI
PS-5	Personnel Transfer	CUI
PS-6	Access Agreements	NFO
PS-7	Third-Party Personnel Security	NFO
PS-8	Personnel Sanctions	NFO

TABLE E-14: TAILORING ACTIONS FOR RISK ASSESSMENT CONTROLS

NIST SP 800-53 MODERATE BASELINE SECURITY CONTROLS		TAILORING ACTION
RA-1	Risk Assessment Policy and Procedures	NFO
RA-2	Security Categorization	FED
RA-3	Risk Assessment	CUI
RA-5	Vulnerability Scanning	CUI
RA-5(1)	VULNERABILITY SCANNING | UPDATE TOOL CAPABILITY	NFO
RA-5(2)	VULNERABILITY SCANNING | UPDATE BY FREQUENCY / PRIOR TO NEW SCAN / WHEN IDENTIFIED	NFO
RA-5(5)	VULNERABILITY SCANNING | PRIVILEGED ACCESS	CUI

TABLE E-15: TAILORING ACTIONS FOR SYSTEM AND SERVICES ACQUISITION CONTROLS[42]

	NIST SP 800-53 MODERATE BASELINE SECURITY CONTROLS	TAILORING ACTION
SA-1	System and Services Acquisition Policy and Procedures	NFO
SA-2	Allocation of Resources	NFO
SA-3	System Development Life Cycle	NFO
SA-4	Acquisition Process	NFO
SA-4(1)	*ACQUISITION PROCESS | FUNCTIONAL PROPERTIES OF SECURITY CONTROLS*	NFO
SA-4(2)	*ACQUISITION PROCESS | DESIGN / IMPLEMENTATION INFORMATION FOR SECURITY CONTROLS*	NFO
SA-4(9)	*ACQUISITION PROCESS | FUNCTIONS / PORTS / PROTOCOLS / SERVICES IN USE*	NFO
SA-4(10)	*ACQUISITION PROCESS | USE OF APPROVED PIV PRODUCTS*	NFO
SA-5	System Documentation	NFO
SA-8	Security Engineering Principles	CUI
SA-9	External System Services	NFO
SA-9(2)	*EXTERNAL SYSTEMS | IDENTIFICATION OF FUNCTIONS / PORTS / PROTOCOLS / SERVICES*	NFO
SA-10	Developer Configuration Management	NFO
SA-11	Developer Security Testing and Evaluation	NFO

---

[42] SA-8 is grouped with the security controls in the *System and Communications Protection* family in Appendix D since the *System and Services Acquisition* family was not included in the security requirements.

TABLE E-16: TAILORING ACTIONS FOR SYSTEM AND COMMUNICATIONS PROTECTION CONTROLS

	NIST SP 800-53 MODERATE BASELINE SECURITY CONTROLS	TAILORING ACTION
SC-1	System and Communications Protection Policy and Procedures	NFO
SC-2	Application Partitioning	CUI
SC-4	Information in Shared Resources	CUI
SC-5	Denial of Service Protection	NCO
SC-7	Boundary Protection	CUI
SC-7(3)	BOUNDARY PROTECTION | ACCESS POINTS	NFO
SC-7(4)	BOUNDARY PROTECTION | EXTERNAL TELECOMMUNICATIONS SERVICES	NFO
SC-7(5)	BOUNDARY PROTECTION | DENY BY DEFAULT / ALLOW BY EXCEPTION	CUI
SC-7(7)	BOUNDARY PROTECTION | PREVENT SPLIT TUNNELING FOR REMOTE DEVICES	CUI
SC-8	Transmission Confidentiality and Integrity	CUI
SC-8(1)	TRANSMISSION CONFIDENTIALITY AND INTEGRITY | CRYPTOGRAPHIC OR ALTERNATE PHYSICAL PROTECTION	CUI
SC-10	Network Disconnect	CUI
SC-12	Cryptographic Key Establishment and Management	CUI
SC-13	Cryptographic Protection	CUI
SC-15	Collaborative Computing Devices	CUI
SC-17	Public Key Infrastructure Certificates	FED
SC-18	Mobile Code	CUI
SC-19	Voice over Internet Protocol	CUI
SC-20	Secure Name /Address Resolution Service (Authoritative Source)	NFO
SC-21	Secure Name /Address Resolution Service (Recursive or Caching Resolver)	NFO
SC-22	Architecture and Provisioning for Name/Address Resolution Service	NFO
SC-23	Session Authenticity	CUI
SC-28	Protection of Information at Rest	CUI
SC-39	Process Isolation	NFO

TABLE E-17: TAILORING ACTIONS FOR SYSTEM AND INFORMATION INTEGRITY CONTROLS

	NIST SP 800-53 MODERATE BASELINE SECURITY CONTROLS	TAILORING ACTION
SI-1	System and Information Integrity Policy and Procedures	NFO
SI-2	Flaw Remediation	CUI
SI-2(2)	*FLAW REMEDIATION	AUTOMATED FLAW REMEDIATION STATUS*	NCO
SI-3	Malicious Code Protection	CUI
SI-3(1)	*MALICIOUS CODE PROTECTION	CENTRAL MANAGEMENT*	NCO
SI-3(2)	*MALICIOUS CODE PROTECTION	AUTOMATIC UPDATES*	NCO
SI-4	System Monitoring	CUI
SI-4(2)	*SYSTEM MONITORING	AUTOMATED TOOLS FOR REAL-TIME ANALYSIS*	NCO
SI-4(4)	*SYSTEM MONITORING	INBOUND AND OUTBOUND COMMUNICATIONS TRAFFIC*	CUI
SI-4(5)	*SYSTEM MONITORING	SYSTEM-GENERATED ALERTS*	NFO
SI-5	Security Alerts, Advisories, and Directives	CUI
SI-7	Software, Firmware, and Information Integrity	NCO
SI-7(1)	*SOFTWARE, FIRMWARE, AND INFORMATION INTEGRITY	INTEGRITY CHECKS*	NCO
SI-7(7)	*SOFTWARE, FIRMWARE, AND INFORMATION INTEGRITY	INTEGRATION OF DETECTION AND RESPONSE*	NCO
SI-8	Spam Protection	NCO
SI-8(1)	*SPAM PROTECTION	CENTRAL MANAGEMENT*	NCO
SI-8(2)	*SPAM PROTECTION	AUTOMATIC UPDATES*	NCO
SI-10	Information Input Validation	NCO
SI-11	Error Handling	NCO
SI-12	Information Handling and Retention	FED
SI-16	Memory Protection	NFO

FORWARD/COMMENTARY

The National Institute of Standards and Technology (NIST) is a measurement standards laboratory, and a non-regulatory agency of the United States Department of Commerce. Its mission is to promote innovation and industrial competitiveness. Founded in 1901, as the National Bureau of Standards, NIST was formed with the mandate to provide standard weights and measures, and to serve as the national physical laboratory for the United States. With a world-class measurement and testing laboratory encompassing a wide range of areas of computer science, mathematics, statistics, and systems engineering, NIST's cybersecurity program supports its overall mission to promote U.S. innovation and industrial competitiveness by advancing measurement science, standards, and related technology through research and development in ways that enhance economic security and improve our quality of life.

The need for cybersecurity standards and best practices that address interoperability, usability and privacy has been shown to be critical for the nation. NIST's cybersecurity programs seek to enable greater development and application of practical, innovative security technologies and methodologies that enhance the country's ability to address current and future computer and information security challenges.

The cybersecurity publications produced by NIST cover a wide range of cybersecurity concepts that are carefully designed to work together to produce a holistic approach to cybersecurity primarily for government agencies and constitute the best practices used by industry. This holistic strategy to cybersecurity covers the gamut of security subjects from development of secure encryption standards for communication and storage of information while at rest to how best to recover from a cyber-attack.

Why buy a book you can download for free?   We print this so you don't have to.

Some are available only in electronic media. Some online docs are missing pages or barely legible.

We at 4th Watch Publishing are former government employees, so we know how government employees actually use the standards. When a new standard is released, an engineer prints it out, punches holes and puts it in a 3-ring binder. While this is not a big deal for a 5 or 10-page document, many NIST documents are over 100 pages and printing a large document is a time-consuming effort. So, an engineer that's paid $75 an hour is spending hours simply printing out the tools needed to do the job. That's time that could be better spent doing engineering. We publish these documents so engineers can focus on what they were hired to do – engineering. It's much more cost-effective to just order the latest version from Amazon.com

If there is a standard you would like published, let us know. Our web site is usgovpub.com

Many of our titles are available as eBooks for Kindle, iPad, Nook, remarkable, BOOX, and Sony eReaders. Buy the paperback from Amazon and get Kindle eBook FREE using MATCHBOOK. Go to https://usgovpub.com to learn more.

Why buy an eBook when you can access data on a website for free? HYPERLINKS

Yes, many books are available as a PDF, but not all PDFs are bookmarked? Do you really want to search a 6,500-page PDF document manually? Load our copy onto your Kindle, PC, iPad, Android Tablet, Nook, or iPhone (download the FREE kindle App from the APP Store) and you have an easily searchable copy. Most devices will allow you to easily navigate an ePub to any Chapter. Note that there is a distinction between a Table of Contents and "Page Navigation". Page Navigation refers to a different sort of Table of Contents. Not one appearing as a page in the book, but one that shows up on the device itself when the reader accesses the navigation feature. Readers can click on a navigation link to jump to a Chapter or Subchapter. Once there, most devices allow you to "pinch and zoom" in or out to easily read the text. (Unfortunately, downloading the free sample file at Amazon.com does not include this feature. You have to buy a copy to get that functionality, but as inexpensive as eBooks are, it's worth it.) Kindle allows you to do word search and Page Flip (temporary place holder takes you back when you want to go back and check something). Visit **USGOVPUB.COM** to learn more.